English for Mass Communication

— 2021 Edition —

Hirofumi Horie
Kaori Kato
Kazuhisa Konishi
Shuji Miyazaki
Yasuko Uchino

ASAHI PRESS

音声再生アプリ「リスニング・トレーナー」を使った 音声ダウンロード

朝日出版社開発のアプリ、「リスニング・トレーナー（リストレ）」を使えば、教科書の音声を スマホ、タブレットに簡単にダウンロードできます。どうぞご活用ください。

◉ アプリ【リスニング・トレーナー】の使い方

《アプリのダウンロード》

App Store または Google Play から 「リスニング・トレーナー」のアプリ （無料）をダウンロード

App Store は こちら▶

Google Play は こちら▶

《アプリの使い方》

① アプリを開き「コンテンツを追加」をタップ
② 画面上部に【15665】を入力し Done をタップ

音声ストリーミング配信 》》》

この教科書の音声は、 右記ウェブサイトにて 無料で配信しています。

https://text.asahipress.com/free/english/

記事提供：CNN / The Japan Times / NIKKEI ASIAN REVIEW / Reuters / The Economist / VOA News / The Wall Street Journal / 朝日新聞社 / 共同通信社 / AP / AFP / 毎日新聞社 / 読売新聞社

写真提供：AP / CNN / iStock /KRT / The New York Times / アフロ / ロイター / AFP / WAA

表紙デザイン：大下賢一郎
本文イラスト：駿高泰子

は　し　が　き

　この本は、新聞・放送の英語ニュースをできるだけ多角的に学べるように編集したものです。

　時事英語を学ぶという行為は、「時事英語を理解すること」と「時事的な事柄や問題に関して英語でコミュニケーションを行うこと」の二つを学ぶことです。英語を読んだり、聞いたりすることは前者であり、時事的な事柄や問題に関して英語で書いたり、話したりすることが後者です。学習の順序としては、いうまでもなく、「理解」から入っていかなければなりません。英字新聞を読めず、英語放送を聞いてもよくわからない人が満足な英語を書けるはずがありませんし、話すことも期待できません。

　従って、この本の編集上の重点は、当然、「理解力の向上」に置かれています。この本では、政治・経済・外交・軍事・環境からスポーツにいたるまで多方面の英語ニュースを理解していただくように編集してあります。この教科書には授業の組み立て方に沿って色々な使い方があると思います。例えば、最もオーソドックスな使い方としては、まず時事英語の「理解力向上」に向けて二段階のアプローチをとることが可能です。まず第一段階として、英語ニュースを時事日本語に移しかえる能力を養うことです。そして第二段階でニュースの基本用語と英語ニュースの語学的特質を理解することです。従って、本書では各章において、まず、英語ニュースの読解と翻訳を行う構成となっています。そして、EXERCISE は、基本語学力を向上させることをねらいとしていますが、できるだけ「生きた英語」にアプローチしてもらうよう編集してあります。THE WORLD OF ENGLISH JOURNALISM は、主としてニュース英語の世界やニュース英語の語学的特質の理解を深めていただくために設けられています。また VOCABULARY BUILDUP は語彙力の充実をはかることをねらいとしています。この他にもいくつかの使い方があると思います。それぞれの授業の目標に即して最適な方法でお使い頂ければと思います。

　なお、本書における英語の綴りや句読点は、原則として、オリジナル記事の綴りに準拠しました。米国式・英国式で綴り方に違いがある場合も原文記事のままとし、必要に応じ注を加えてあります。例えば、「アメリカ合衆国」の略称は、米国式では U.S. となり、英国式では US となりますが、原文のままとしています。また、ニュース記事の冒頭における発信地の明示についても、内外のニュースを問わずオリジナル記事に準拠しました。

　本書の内容を一層充実させるため、読者諸氏のご教示を頂ければ幸いです。

　最後に、本書の出版にあたり種々のお骨折りを頂いた朝日出版社の日比野忠氏、加藤愛理氏、田所メアリー氏にこの場を借りて厚く御礼申し上げます。

編　著　者

CONTENTS

English for Mass Communication

NEWS 1
Japan to lift coronavirus state of emergency for Tokyo

Disk 1
2

Japanese Prime Minister Shinzo Abe has lifted the state of emergency for Tokyo and four neighboring prefectures imposed last month at the height of the coronavirus outbreak. The move ends nationwide restrictions as businesses begin to reopen their doors.

The prime minister announced the move Monday during a televised speech, 5 hours after a special coronavirus panel approved a plan to lift the decree for the Japanese capital and its surrounding areas. The decision was made after the number of new infections began trending downward

The prime minister initially declared a 30-day state of emergency on April 7 for Tokyo and six other prefectures, including the central port city of Osaka, as the 10 number of COVID-19 infections began to rise.

Prime Minister Abe extended the measure nationwide just a few days before it was set to expire, then gradually lifted it as the outbreak appeared to ease. The decree was set to expire on May 31.

3 The emergency declaration stopped short of imposing a legally binding 15 nationwide lockdown, due to Japan's post-World War II constitution, which weighs heavily in favor of civil liberties.

Japan currently has more than 16,500 confirmed cases of COVID-19 infections with 820 deaths, a relatively low figure compared with other nations. Abe said Monday that the country's success in containing the coronavirus in such a short 20 period of time showed the strength of the "Japan model."

The outbreak, however, has pushed the Japanese economy into a recession and forced postponement of the Tokyo Summer Olympic Games for a year. Abe's approval ratings have also plunged to record lows due to his apparent slow response to the pandemic. 25

— Based on a report on VOANews.com on May 25, 2020 —

〈ニュース解説〉　新型コロナウイルスが世界的な感染拡大を見せる中、日本政府は水際対策に注力してきたが、一般国民の感染症例が増大し、医療体制ひっ迫の懸念も高まったことから、2020年4月緊急事態宣言を発出した。国民の自主的な外出自粛や企業のテレワーク導入、学校の閉鎖等が奏功し、5月25日、宣言は解除された。だが、感染防止措置の影響を受けた事業者への対策は限られたものとなり、世界経済の減速の影響もあって経済の低迷は不可避となった。さらに、宣言解除後、大都市圏を中心に起きた感染再燃の動きも事態を不透明にさせた。

(Notes)

◆ **Japan to lift coronavirus state of emergency for Tokyo**　「日本　東京の新型コロナウイルス緊急事態宣言解除へ」［"coronavirus state of emergency" 正式名称は「新型コロナウイルス感染症緊急事態宣言」2020年4月7日、政府は、新型コロナウイルスのまん延が国民生活及び国民経済に甚大な影響を及ぼすおそれがあるとして、新型インフルエンザ等対策特別措置法（略称「新型コロナ特措法」）に基づき、東京、埼玉、千葉、神奈川、大阪、兵庫及び福岡の7都府県を対象に同宣言を発出、給付金支給や雇用確保等の経済対策も決定した。さらに同16日、対象を日本全国に広げ、北海道、茨城、石川、岐阜、愛知及び京都の6道府県を特定警戒都道府県に位置付けた。5月2日、対象期限は5月31日まで延長されたが、感染が下火傾向となったため、5月25日に前倒しで解除された。英語ニュースの見出し "headline" は、本記事のように冒頭段落の "lead" を要約する場合や記事内容から新たに書き下ろす場合がある。即時性と簡潔さを尊び、過去の事象にも現在形を用いる、冠詞を省略する等、独特のスタイルがある。なお、P.13 "THE WORLD OF ENGLISH JOURNALISM（The headline）" 参照のこと］

◆ (L. 1)　**Japanese Prime Minister Shinzo Abe**　安倍晋三首相（英語ニュースでは "prime minister" の代替表現として中国やイタリア、フランス、ロシアで首相を表す "premier" も使われる）

◆ (L. 2)　**four neighboring prefectures**　（東京）近隣の4県（埼玉、神奈川、千葉及び茨城を指す）

◆ (L. 3)　**outbreak**　感染症の急激な拡大（アウトブレイク）

◆ (L. 3)　**businesses**　経済界（一般企業から飲食、観光、サービスまで影響を受けた産業全体を指す）

◆ (L. 5)　**televised speech**　テレビ中継による（記者会見での）演説

◆ (L. 6)　**special coronavirus panel**　コロナウイルス感染症に関する政府専門家会合

◆ (L. 6)　**the decree**　［"decree" は法令に基づく命令や宣言の意。ここでは緊急事態宣言を指す。新型コロナ特措法は2012年制定の新型インフルエンザ等対策特別措置法を改正し、対象に新型コロナウイルス感染症を加えたもの（2020年3月13日成立）。同法に基づき緊急事態宣言が出されると、国や地方公共団体は行動計画を作成する。都道府県知事は、住民に対する外出制限要請、興行場や催物等の制限等の要請・指示、医療提供体制の確保等を行うほか、臨時医療施設開設のため、土地や建物を権利者の同意なしに強制使用することも可能となる］

◆ (L. 6-7)　**the Japanese capital and its surrounding areas**　（日本の）首都東京とその周辺地域

◆ (L. 7-8)　**the number of new infections**　新規感染者数

◆ (L. 10)　**central port city of Osaka**　大阪（"of" は同格を表す。直訳は「日本中央部の港湾都市である大阪」で大阪市をイメージしているが、緊急事態宣言の対象は大阪府であった）

◆ (L. 11)　**COVID-19**　新型コロナウイルス（感染症）［「2019年新型コロナウイルス感染症 "Coronavirus Disease 2019"」の略称。世界保健機関（WHO）が命名］

◆ (L. 12-13)　**a few days before it was set to expire**　当初の期限が切れる数日前に

◆ (L. 15-16)　**a legally binding nationwide lockdown**　法的強制力を持つ全国的ロックダウン（都市封鎖）（日本国憲法には緊急事態における私権制限に関する規定がなく、不可能とされている）

◆ (L. 16)　**Japan's post-World War II constitution**　第二次世界大戦後に制定された日本の憲法

◆ (L. 21)　**"Japan model"**　「日本モデル」（諸外国が都市封鎖などの強硬手段をとったのに対し、強制力のない要請のみで感染拡大を防ごうとしたやり方）

◆ (L. 23)　**the Tokyo Summer Olympic Games**　夏季オリンピック（2020年）東京大会（パラリンピック東京大会ともども1年間延期された）

◆ (L. 23-24)　**Abe's approval ratings**　安倍内閣支持率（検事総長の定年延長への批判も加わり、各世論調査で40パーセントを切った）

◆ (L. 25)　**pandemic**　パンデミック、世界的な感染拡大［"pan-" は「汎」、「広がりを持つ」を意味する接頭辞。「流行病」を意味する "epidemic" の "epi-（一点の）" の代わりに使われている］

ニュースを読んで、下記の設問に答えよ。

1. 本文の内容と一致するものには T (True) を、一致しないものには F (False) を記せ。

( ) (1) Prime Minister Shinzo Abe lifted the coronavirus state of emergency for Tokyo and four neighboring prefectures, but kept the nationwide restrictions intact.

( ) (2) Mr Abe announced his decision to lift the state of emergency, considering that the number of new infections began trending downward.

( ) (3) Prime Minister Abe issued a second declaration after the first decree had expired.

( ) (4) Regardless of the post-World War II constitution, Japan's emergency declaration is legally entitled to lock down whole areas affected by the coronavirus.

( ) (5) When Mr Abe lifted the restrictions, the confirmed numbers of COVID-19 infections and the number of deaths in Japan were relatively low compared with other countries.

( ) (6) The COVID-19 outbreak has pushed the country's economy into a recession but has had no adverse effect on the schedule of the Olympics in 2020.

( ) (7) Prime Minister Abe's approval ratings have plummeted to the lowest level because of his prompt actions against the pandemic.

2. 次の英文を完成させるために、(a) 〜 (d) から最も適切なものを 1 つ選べ。

Japanese Prime Minister Shinzo Abe finally declared the termination of the coronavirus state of emergency on May 25, having maintained the decree for
_____

(a) more than 50 days.

(b) just 50 days.

(c) less than 50 days.

(d) (Unable to specify)

natural
4
slow
6

Yuriko Koike was re-elected Tokyo governor on Sunday, (1) _____ _____ released by public broadcaster NHK, after winning over voters with her handling of the COVID-19 pandemic in the Japanese capital.

Koike's victory in the city that will host the Olympic Games next year had been widely expected, even though it confirmed 111 new coronavirus infections on Sunday, the fourth successive day that (2) _____ _____ 100.　　　　　　　　　　5

"Our urgent task, above everything else, is our coronavirus response," Koike, who became Tokyo's first woman governor in 2016 and has won (3) _____ _____ the coronavirus, said after NHK called her election win.　　10

natural
5
slow
7

The metropolis accounts for 11 percent of Japan's population, but has represented half of the country's daily infections in recent weeks.

Koike, 67, will face a difficult task of trying to curb the coronavirus (4) _____ _____ in the capital, which accounts for about 20 percent of Japan's economy.　　　　　　　　　　15

Koike, (5) _____ _____, will also be the face of the host city of the next Olympics, which had been scheduled to start this month but were postponed by a year because of the coronavirus.

— *Based on a report on Reuters.com on July 5, 2020* —

〈ニュース解説〉　2016 年、「都民ファースト」をスローガンに初の女性東京都知事に選ばれた小池百合子氏。将来の首相候補と噂され、知事就任後も 2017 年の衆議院議員総選挙において当時の民進党分裂のきっかけを作る台風の目となった。2020 年の東京オリンピック・パラリンピック開催を踏み台に国政復帰を目指すのではないかと言われたが、折からの新型コロナ対策に全力投球するとして 2 期目の選挙に臨み、歴代 2 位の記録となる 366 万票余を獲得、再選された。

(Notes)
Yuriko Koike 小池百合子　**Tokyo governor** 東京都知事　**public broadcaster NHK** 公共放送の NHK［正式名称「日本放送協会（Japan Broadcasting Corporation）」。NHK は "Nippon Hoso Kyokai" の頭文字からとった「公称」。放送法により設立された特殊法人で、国営（state-owned）ではないが、事業計画、予・決算は国会承認を必要とする］
fourth successive day 連続 4 日目　**the metropolis** 首都東京（機関としての東京都を表す英語名称は "Tokyo Metropolitan Government" という）　**daily infections** 毎日の感染者数　**curb** 抑制する　**host city of the next Olympics** 次期オリンピック開催都市

■問A　空所 (a) 〜 (n) にそれぞれ入るべき 1 語を下記の語群から選びその番号を記せ。

内閣府	→	Cabinet (a)
防衛省	→	Ministry of (b)
金融庁	→	Financial Services (c)
法務省	→	Ministry of (d)
総務省	→	Ministry of Internal Affairs and (e)
財務省	→	Ministry of (f)
外務省	→	Ministry of Foreign (g)
環境省	→	Ministry of the (h)
文部科学省	→	Ministry of (i), Culture, Sports, Science and Technology
厚生労働省	→	Ministry of (j), Labour, and Welfare
農林水産省	→	Ministry of Agriculture, Forestry and (k)
経済産業省	→	Ministry of Economy, (l) and Industry
国土交通省	→	Ministry of Land, (m), Transport and Tourism
国家公安委員会	→	National Public Safety (n)

> 1. Affairs　　　　2. Agency　　　　3. Commission
> 4. Communications　5. Defense　　　6. Education
> 7. Environment　　8. Finance　　　9. Fisheries
> 10. Health　　　11. Infrastructure　12. Justice
> 13. Office　　　14. Trade

■問B　(a) 〜 (f) にそれぞれ対応する英語表現を下記の語群から選びその番号を記せ。

(a) 憲法　　(b) 国会　　(c) 総選挙　　(d) 与党　　(e) 野党　　(f) 連立

> 1. coalition　　　　2. constitution　　　3. Diet
> 4. general election　5. opposition party　6. ruling party

■問C　空所 (a) 〜 (j) にそれぞれ入るべき 1 語を下記の語群から選びその番号を記せ。

自由民主党	→ (a) Democratic Party	立憲民主党	→ (b) Democratic Party of Japan
公明党	→ (c) Party	日本維新の会	→ Nippon (d) no Kai
日本共産党	→ Japanese (e) Party	国民民主党	→ Democratic Party for the (f)
小選挙区制	→ single-seat (g) system	比例代表制	→ proportional (h) system
衆議院	→ House of (i)	参議院	→ House of (j)

> 1. Communist　　2. constituency　3. Constitutional　4. Councillors
> 5. Ishin　　　　6. Komeito　　　7. Liberal　　　8. People
> 9. representation　10. Representatives

News defined ― ニュースは記者が決める？

掲載するニュースを決めるのは編集局（記者）だが、ニュースの定義には、世の中に起こっているすべてがニュースだという考えもある。しかし他方で、そのような様々な出来事からニュースにする価値あり（newsworthy）と記者が判断して選んだものがニュースだという考えもある。記者たちの中には、"We determine the news!" と公言して、ニュースは記者が作るものだと考えている人たちも多い。また、ニュースを選ぶ基準として、"what people want to know" と "what people need to know" の間のバランスを取ることも大切である。

このトピックを英文で読んでみよう。

　　How do you determine whether a current idea, event or problem is news? How do you recognize it, separating swiftly the news and the non-news in what happens? How can you be sure that it will interest readers, listeners, or viewers?

　　To answer these questions, examine the elements common in all news. These may also be termed news values, appeals, factors, determinants, or criteria. Even if one is missing, the reporter may question whether the happening is news.

　　The five news elements are: (a) timeliness, (b) nearness, (c) size, (d) importance and (e) personal benefit.

NEWS 2

Disk 1

8

IMF downgrades already-glum economic outlook due to coronavirus crisis

Economists at the International Monetary Fund now say the global economy will contract even more sharply than they expected in estimates released in April, which called for the steepest recession since the Great Depression.

The IMF said on Wednesday the global economy will shrink 4.9% this year, compared with its April estimate of 3%. The international lending institution 5 downgraded its 2020 forecast for all major economies, citing economic data that was even grimmer than expected in April.

Most countries are beginning to emerge from the lockdowns imposed around much of the world beginning in March to stem the spread of the novel coronavirus. And, in many cases, there are encouraging signs that large numbers of workers are 10 returning to work and economic activity is stabilizing or even picking up. But, in sum, the world has made less progress than expected in April in terms of combating the pandemic and salvaging businesses, and so the forecasts have deteriorated.

9 "The steep decline in activity comes with a catastrophic hit to the global labor market," the IMF said in an update to its flagship World Economic Outlook report 15 that analyzes the economic health of the IMF's 189 member countries. The IMF said global employment loss in the second quarter of 2020 could be equivalent to losing 300 million full-time jobs.

Though the current decline appears significantly worse than anything since the Great Depression, it isn't nearly as bad as that downturn, which began in 1929. 20 During that episode, the global economy shrunk by 10% over three years—compared with this year's 4.9% forecast. Advanced economies contracted by around 16% then, compared with the 8% expected for this year.

In contrast to the Great Depression, from which the world struggled to recover for a decade, the IMF expects the global economy to grow in 2021 and said that, on a 25 monthly basis, many countries may have passed the worst.

"Where economies have been reopening, activity may have troughed in April," the IMF said.

Among the hardest hit economies are the U.S., which is forecast to shrink 8% this year. The IMF estimates the euro-area economy will contract by 10.2%, Brazil 30 by 9.1%, Mexico by 10.5%, and the U.K. by 10.2%. China is expected to be the only major economy to expand in 2020, but even their growth is forecast to be just 1%.

— Based on a report on WSJ.com on June 24, 2020 —

〈ニュース解説〉 2019年の世界の実質GDP成長率3％（推定）を受けて、国際通貨基金 (IMF) は2020年1月に20年の成長率を3.3％、21年は3.4％と予測した。しかし、4月には新型コロナウイルスの全世界感染者数が100万人、死者が5万人を上回り、20年の予測をマイナス3％、21年は感染の封じ込めと経済活動の再開を想定して＋5.8％に修正した。6月後半に至ると感染者が1000万人、死者が50万人を超え、本ニュースが伝えるように再度、成長見通しを修正した。感染封じ込めの決め手となるワクチンや治療薬が開発途上の中、感染第2波が拡大した場合には世界経済はさらに深刻な局面を迎えることになる。

(Notes)

◆ **IMF**　国際通貨基金（International Monetary Fund。国際金融と為替相場の安定化を目指す国連の専門機関。2019年3月現在の加盟国189か国。本部：米ワシントン D.C.）

◆ **downgrade**　格下げする、下方修正する

◆ **glum**　陰鬱な、不景気な

◆ (L. 2)　**contract**　縮小する

◆ (L. 3)　**call for . . .**　予測する（主に天気予報で用いられる表現）

◆ (L. 3)　**Great Depression**　大恐慌、世界恐慌［1929年10月24日にニューヨーク証券取引所で株価が暴落したことに端を発し、1930年代に全世界に波及した経済危機。1920年代の米国は、第1次世界大戦後の復興需要や自動車などの新産業の勃興により好景気に沸いていたが、その結果バブルが発生した。景気は1933年3月に一旦底打ちするが、1937年に再び厳しい後退局面に入り、米国経済が正常な状態に戻ったのは1940年頃とされ、約10年にわたり世界規模の深刻な不況と大量失業に見舞われた。だが、この後、欧米諸国が保護主義やブロック経済化に陥ったため、世界貿易の大幅な縮小をもたらしたことが、第二次世界大戦の遠因になったとされる］

◆ (L. 5)　**international lending institution**　（IMFを指している。国際収支が著しく悪化した加盟国に通貨の貸付を実施することがIMFの重要な役割の一つ）

◆ (L. 13)　**business**　企業、ビジネス、事業

◆ (L. 14)　**come with . . .**　. . . を伴う

◆ (L. 15)　**flagship World Economic Outlook**　旗艦レポート『世界経済見通し』（略称 "WEO"。IMFが通常毎年4月と10月に発表し、7月と翌年1月にアップデート版を出しているが、2020年は6月に繰り上げ発表された）

◆ (L. 18)　**full-time job**　フルタイム雇用（ほぼ「正規雇用」を指す）

◆ (L. 22)　**advanced economies**　先進国経済

◆ (L. 27)　**trough**　底を打つ

◆ (L. 30)　**euro-area economy**　ユーロ圏経済［欧州連合（EU）の内、欧州統一通貨「ユーロ」を導入している国で形成される経済圏。2020年1月現在で19カ国］

ニュースを読んで、下記の設問に答えよ。

1. 本文の内容と一致するものには T (True) を、一致しないものには F (False) を記せ。

(　) (1) The IMF now believes that in April, the global economy will suffer the worst economic downturn since the Great Depression.

(　) (2) The IMF earlier predicted that the global economy would shrink in April by only 3%.

(　) (3) Starting in March, many countries started taking emergency measures to stop the coronavirus from spreading.

(　) (4) The IMF has lowered its forecast for the global economy because most countries have not made as much progress as expected in tackling the pandemic.

(　) (5) The IMF has updated its forecast for the global economy by analyzing the economies of its members.

2. 次の英文を完成させるために、(a) ～ (d) から最も適切なものを 1 つ選べ。

(1) According to the IMF, the economic decline caused by the novel coronavirus is likely to be far smaller than that caused by the Great Depression, because _____

(a) the current downturn is likely to be shorter and less devastating.

(b) the Great Depression created full-time job losses of 300 million.

(c) the current downturn is affecting poor countries more seriously.

(d) the Great Depression caused far more serious psychological effects.

(2) The IMF forecasts that the global economy will start growing in 2021 because _____

(a) many economies now appear to have put the worst behind them on a monthly basis.

(b) the U.S. economy is predicted to contract only by 8% this year.

(c) major economies in the euro area are expected to grow significantly in 2021.

(d) indications are that China's growth will accelerate in 2021.

Natural
10
Slow
12

Getting the global economy back on its feet this year won't be easy. But it will be even tougher without more help from China, the locomotive that powered recoveries from the world's last economic emergency.

During the 2008-09 financial crisis, China's soaring demand for raw materials and other goods boosted growth across the world, (1) _____ 5
_____ Brazil and Germany. Some countries, like Australia, avoided recession almost entirely thanks to trade with China.

China isn't poised to help as much this time. (2) _____
_____ recently, its economy has been hit much harder than in 2008-09, limiting its ability to lift other nations from recession prompted by the coronavirus 10 pandemic.

Natural
11
Slow
13

China is showing more restraint on stimulus spending compared with past downturns. It is also (3) _____ than previously, meaning it may need to buy less from abroad.

Thomas Nuernberger, Greater China chief executive of ebm-papst Group, 15 a fan and motor manufacturer based in southern Germany, says demand from Chinese hospitals and data centers has recovered. But sales have fallen sharply to the auto industry and to Chinese manufacturers that ship their products elsewhere. He (4) _____ and businesses to weigh on growth, reducing odds of a "V-shaped" recovery. 20

"For 2020 it is not possible, I think, that China does the job it did in 2008-09," said Thilo Brodtmann, executive director of the German Mechanical Engineering Industry Association, a trade body. "Quite a few companies in China are struggling."

China is the only major economy forecast to grow in 2020. But it isn't 25 expected to lift other countries as much as during the last recession, when Chinese demand (5) _____ .

— *Based on a report on WSJ.com on July 12, 2020* —

〈ニュース解説〉　中国経済は新型コロナウイルスの感染拡大を受けて、2020 年第１四半期（１～３月）は実質 GDP 成長率が対前年同期比で 6.8％減と記録的なマイナス成長となった。一方、第２四半期にはウイルス禍を抑え込み、先進経済国に先駆けて 3.2％のプラス成長を達成した。しかし、雇用や個人消費の回復が遅れており、2008～09 年のリーマン・ショック時のように世界経済を牽引する力強さはないと見られている。

(Notes)

2008-09 financial crisis（2007 年に米国で住宅バブルが崩壊し、同国投資銀行リーマン・ブラザーズが 2008 年９月に経営破綻、連鎖的に世界規模の金融危機が発生した。前段落の the world's last economic emergency と同義で、日本では「リーマンショック」と呼ばれることが多い）　**stimulus spending** 財政刺激策　**Thomas Nuernberger** トーマス・ニューエンバーガー（Ebm-papst グループの中華圏経営責任者）　**"V-shaped" recovery** Ｖ字（型）回復　**Thilo Brodtmann** ティロ・ブロッドマン（ドイツ機械装置産業連盟の代表）

■問A　空所 (a) ～ (s) にそれぞれ入るべき 1 語を下記の語群から選びその番号を記せ。

国内総生産	→	(a) domestic product
消費者物価指数	→	(b) price index
卸売物価指数	→	(c) price index
非関税障壁	→	non-tariff (d)
最恵国	→	most (e) nation
政府開発援助	→	(f) development assistance
貿易不均衡	→	trade (g)
為替レート	→	(h) rate
国際収支	→	(i) of international payments
経常収支	→	current (j)
貿易自由化	→	trade (k)
社会保障	→	social (l)
企業の合併・買収	→	(m) and acquisition
株式公開買い付け	→	(n) bid
店頭取引株	→	over-the-(o) stock
優良株	→	(p) chip
不良債権	→	(q) loan
失業率	→	(r) rate
住宅着工件数	→	(s) starts

1. account	2. bad	3. balance	4. barrier
5. blue	6. consumer	7. counter	8. exchange
9. favored	10. gross	11. housing	12. imbalance
13. jobless	14. liberalization	15. merger	16. official
17. security	18. takeover	19. wholesale	

■問B　(a) ～ (d) をそれぞれ和訳せよ。

(a) European Central Bank
(b) Bank of Japan
(c) Federal Reserve Board
(d) New York Stock Exchange

■問C　(a) ～ (d) にそれぞれ対応する英語を下記の語群から選びその番号を記せ。

(a) 景気後退　　(b) 好況　　(c) 倒産　　(d) 年金

1. bankruptcy	2. bonus	3. boom	4. breakdown
5. pension	6. recession	7. rehabilitation	

The headline ―「見出し」の特徴

現代英文ジャーナリズムの「見出し」（headline）では、日常的に用いられない語を「見出し語」（headlinese）として使用することを避ける傾向が強い。見出しは記事の内容を簡潔明瞭に表現する必要があり、一般的に次の5つの特徴を有している。

（1）略語が多い。例えば、"GOP" と言えば "Grand Old Party" の略称で、米国共和党（Republican Party）の異名。

（2）特殊記号がある。例えば、"and" をカンマで代用したり、情報源を表すコロンがある。ヘッドラインのコロンはすべて情報源を表すものではないが、"Gunman in Manhattan kills one woman, wounds three: NYPD" とあれば、カンマは "and" に置き換えて "Gunman in Manhattan kills one woman and wounds three" となり、この情報は NYPD（New York City Police Department, ニューヨーク市警察）によってもたらされたことがわかる。

（3）冠詞や be 動詞は省略されることが多い。

（4）見出しにとどまらず、英語ニュースでは、首都名はその国や政府を表すことが多い。例えば、Washington は米国や米国政府を表す場合がよくある。もちろん首都自体のことを表す場合もあるから、文脈に注意。

（5）時制のずらしに気をつけよう。昨日起こったことでも現在形で表現。未来は to 不定詞で表現。例えば見出し語で "Government to regulate the Internet" とあれば、"The government will regulate the Internet" の意味。

このトピックを英文で読んでみよう。

　The modern headline is distinguished by the fact that it says something—it makes a complete statement instead of merely characterizing. But, in addition, it speaks a language of its own. This language is not "headlinese," a perverted speech, but is merely pure English adapted to the requirements of headlining.

　For one thing, the present tense is customarily used to describe past events. This usage is not something created by headline writers, but is simply something borrowed from everyday speech. The present tense is employed because it is the tense of immediacy, because it is more vivid and, hence, because it makes our trial tube of toothpaste inviting to the prospective buyer.

　Another characteristic, which is more obvious to the ordinary reader, is the omission of non-essential words, chiefly articles. This practice has a tendency to give the headline telegraphic speed and, hence, to make it more vivid.

　Still another characteristic of headline language is the use of short words, mainly of Anglo-Saxon derivation. And, here again, the space requirement is the commanding factor.

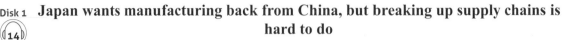

Chapter 3　経済・ビジネス（２）

NEWS 3

Disk 1
(14)
Japan wants manufacturing back from China, but breaking up supply chains is hard to do

Spooked by coronavirus-induced factory shutdowns in China, the Japanese government has earmarked $2 billion to help companies shift production home. The policy, part of a massive stimulus package to cope with the pandemic of the novel coronavirus, has even been termed by some bureaucrats as a matter of national security. 5

"We have become dependent on China," Economy Minister Yasutoshi Nishimura told reporters last week. "We need to make supply chains more robust and diverse, broadening our supply sources and increasing domestic production."

Many Japanese firms say, however, that shifting output back home is simply impractical and uneconomical. They need to be physically present in China because 10 much of what they are making is ultimately for the Chinese consumer, and to meet the demands of 'just-in-time' production which prioritises short delivery times for efficient manufacturing.

(15)
"The parts we make are so big that we need to be near our customers to control our costs," said Chikara Haruta, a spokesman at Yorozu Corp, which makes 15 suspension and other auto components. Its plant in Wuhan, China, is located just seven kilometres from a Honda Motor Co Ltd assembly factory.

For Japan's car makers, reliance on Chinese suppliers in the world's biggest auto market is also just good business. "Even if we wanted to, it would be difficult to lower our exposure to China-made parts," an executive at a Japanese automaker 20 told Reuters, declining to be identified as he was not authorised to speak to media. He added that over the past decade, Chinese suppliers had upped their game and now provide a vast range of quality, low-cost parts.

Toyota Motor Corp, Nissan Motor Co Ltd and Honda also have at least three R&D centres each in China, and their suppliers are following suit. "Where the 25 software is developed dictates where the hardware is developed and made," said an official at a Japanese parts supplier, speaking on condition of anonymity. "The new government incentive is misguided if it only focuses on bringing manufacturing back, while overlooking R&D functions."

— Based on a report on Reuters.com on June 9, 2020 —

〈ニュース解説〉 新型コロナウイルスの感染拡大で内外の経済が急収縮する中、日本政府の緊急経済対策予算は 230 兆円を上回った（2020 年 5 月末現在）。これには、輸入依存のマスクや医療機器などを海外で生産する日本企業に国内回帰を促す補助金 2200 億円が盛り込まれている。補助金は、特定の国への生産依存度が高い製品や素材について、日本国内に工場を新設したり設備を導入したりする場合が対象となっている。自由貿易に基づく国際分業が世界経済の成長力の源泉と見られてきたが、最近では米国を中心に自国優先の保護主義が首をもたげている

(Notes)

◆ **supply chain** サプライチェーン（製品の原材料や部品の調達から製造・在庫管理・配送・販売・消費にいたる一連の流れで、多くの場合、複数の国に立地する複数の企業が役割分担する）

◆ (L. 1) **spook** おびえさせる、怖がらせる

◆ (L. 1) **coronavirus-induced** コロナウイルスにより引き起こされた

◆ (L. 2) **earmark** 取っておく

◆ (L. 2) **billion** 10 億

◆ (L. 3) **stimulus package** 景気刺激策（package は「一括法案」の意）

◆ (L. 4-5) **national security** 国家安全保障

◆ (L. 6) **Economy Minister Yasutoshi Nishimura** 西村康稔経済再生担当大臣（「経済再生担当大臣」の正式英文名称は Minister for Economic Revitalization）

◆ (L. 12) **'just-in-time' production** 「ジャストインタイム」生産システム（生産現場の各工程で「必要な物を、必要な時に、必要な量だけ」供給し、部品在庫を極力最小化するなど効率的な生産を目指すシステムで、トヨタ自動車が考案し、世界に普及した。「トヨタ・かんばん方式」などの呼び名でも有名）

◆ (L. 15) **Chikara Haruta** 春田力

◆ (L. 15) **Yorozu Corp** 株式会社ヨロズ（自動車部品などのメーカー）

◆ (L. 16) **suspension** サスペンション（車両の緩衝装置で乗り心地や操縦安定性を向上）

◆ (L. 16) **Wuhan** 武漢市（中国南部にある湖北省の省都。自動車産業の集積地で大手外資自動車メーカーが進出）

◆ (L. 17) **Honda Motor Co Ltd** 本田技研工業株式会社（通称、「ホンダ」）

◆ (L. 19) **good business** 「会社の利益に資する」［米 IBM が 1960 年代に採用した社内標語 "Good design is good business."（良いデザインは良いビジネスになる）が知られている］

◆ (L. 22) **up one's game** （技能や出来栄えを）改善する

◆ (L. 24) **Toyota Motor Corp** トヨタ自動車株式会社（日本の大手自動車メーカー。通称「トヨタ」）

◆ (L. 24) **Nissan Motor Co Ltd** 日産自動車株式会社（日本の大手自動車メーカー。通称とブランド名は日産）

◆ (L. 25) **R&D centre** 研究開発センター

◆ (L. 25) **follow suit** 追随する（"follow suit" は do the same thing の意）

◆ (L. 27) **on condition of anonymity** 匿名条件で

◆ (L. 28) **misguided** 的外れ、見当違い

1. 本文の内容と一致するものには T (True) を、一致しないものには F (False) を記せ。

(　) (1) The $2 billion government subsidies are designed to help Japanese firms in China to resume production amid the spread of the coronavirus.

(　) (2) A part of the massive stimulus package is aimed at dealing with the pandemic and other national security issues.

(　) (3) Mr Nishimura said that the Japanese economy was so dependent on China that supply chains between the two countries should be further strengthened.

(　) (4) Many Japanese companies in China believe it is most appropriate to make their products where they are consumed.

(　) (5) Yorozu Corp plans to soon move its plant right next to Honda's assembly factory in Wuhan for speedy supply of auto components.

2. 次の英文を完成させるために、(a) ～ (d) から最も適切なものを 1 つ選べ。

(1) According to the news story, one of the reasons that Japanese carmakers in China will maintain local production is _____

(a) the abundant supply of low-cost workers.

(b) the abundant supply of highly trained engineers.

(c) the local availability of various high-quality, low-cost components.

(d) the availability of cheap land on which to expand production.

(2) According to the news story, one of the reasons that Japanese auto parts makers in China will maintain their presence there is _____

(a) the availability of financial incentives from the local government.

(b) the growing size of the local market for auto components.

(c) the importance of closely coordinating R&D and manufacturing in the same market.

(d) the provision of new business incentives from the Japanese government.

Natural **16** / Slow **18**

　　　Toyota Motor Corp said on Monday it planned to build a prototype "city of the future" at the base of Japan's Mt. Fuji, (1) _____ and functioning as a laboratory for autonomous cars, "smart homes," artificial intelligence and other technologies.

　　　Toyota (2) _____ what it will call "Woven City", in a reference to its origins as a loom manufacturer, at the big annual technology industry show, CES. "It's hard to learn something about a smart city if you are only building a smart block," James Kuffner, chief executive officer for the Toyota Research Institute-Advanced Development, told Reuters.　　　5

Natural **17** / Slow **19**

　　　The "Woven City" idea, under discussion for a year, is aimed at creating safer, cleaner, more fun cities and learning lessons that (3) _____, he added. It will have police, fire and ambulance services, schools, and could be home to a mix of Toyota employees, retirees and others, Kuffner said.　　　10

　　　The development, to be built on the site of a car factory that is planned to be closed by the end of 2020, will begin with 2,000 residents in coming years and also serve as a home to researchers. Toyota did not disclose costs for the project, (4) _____ next year, and which seeks to re-imagine a city, but executives said it had been extensively vetted and had a budget.　　　15　　　20

　　　The plan for the futuristic community on 175 acres (71 hectares) is (5) _____ from Toyota's rivals. Executives at many major automakers have talked about how cities of the future could be designed to cut climate-changing emissions, reduce congestion and apply internet technology to everyday life.　　　25

　　　— *Based on a report on Reuters.com on January 7, 2020* —

〈ニュース解説〉　日本が今なお強い国際競争力を誇る産業のひとつ自動車。その代表格トヨタ自動車の豊田章男社長が 2020 年 1 月 7 日、東京・虎ノ門のホテルオークラで開かれた恒例の自動車業界賀詞交歓会を欠席、米ラスベガスの技術見本市「CES」に参加した。目的は、トヨタの「スマートシティー」構想を世界に向けて宣言し、車に関わる総合サービス業への事業転換の第一歩を踏み出すことであった。自動車業界に続々と参入する IT 企業への危機感への表れと見られている。

(Notes)

prototype "city of the future" 実験的「未来都市」　**smart home** スマートホーム（家庭の電化製品をインターネットにつなぎ、スマホや音声などでコントロールし快適な暮らしを実現する家）　**artificial intelligence** 人工知能　**"Woven City"**「ウーブン・シティー」（織り込んだ町）　**CES** [Consumer Electronics Show の略称。毎年 1 月、全米民生技術協会（CTA）が主催し、ネバダ州ラスベガスで開催される電子機器の見本市]　**James Kuffner** ジェームス・カフナー　**chief executive officer** 最高経営責任者（CEO）　**Toyota Research Institute - Advanced Development** トヨタ・リサーチ・インスティテュート・アドバンスト・デベロップメント株式会社（本社：東京）

■問A　空所 (a) 〜 (s) にそれぞれ入るべき 1 語を下記の語群から選びその番号を記せ。

グローバル人材	→ globally (a) human resources
重厚長大産業	→ (b) industry
終身雇用	→ (c) employment
熟練労働者	→ (d) worker
年功序列昇進制度	→ (e)-based promotion system
能力主義昇進制度	→ (f)-based promotion system
食料自給率	→ food (g)-sufficiency rate
初任給	→ (h) salary
人材派遣会社	→ (i)-employment agency
数値目標	→ (j) target
正社員	→ (k) employee
契約社員	→ (l) employee
設備投資	→ (m) investment
先行指標	→ (n) indicator
遅行指標	→ (o) indicator
一致指標	→ (p) indicator
知的所有権	→ intellectual (q) rights
確定給付型年金	→ defined-(r) pension plan
確定拠出型年金	→ defined-(s) pension plan

1. benefit	2. capital	3. coincident	4. competitive
5. contract	6. contribution	7. full–time	8. lagging
9. leading	10. lifetime	11. numerical	12. performance
13. property	14. self	15. seniority	16. skilled
17. smokestack	18. starting	19. temporary	

■問B　(a) 〜 (d) をそれぞれ和訳せよ。

(a) Asian Infrastructure Investment Bank

(b) Government Pension Investment Fund, Japan

(c) Japan External Trade Organization

(d) National Federation of Agricultural Cooperative Associations

■問C　(a) 〜 (d) にそれぞれ対応する英語表現を下記の語群から選びその番号を記せ。

(a) 格安航空会社　　(b) 投資収益率　　(c) 有効求人倍数率　　(d) 連結決算

1. consolidated earnings	2. effective labor force	3. low–cost carrier
4. ratio of job offers to seekers	5. return on investment	6. ultra–low airfare

The inverted pyramid ― 逆ピラミッドとは

英文のニュースの大半は、ハード・ニュース（hard news）と呼ばれ、経済・政治・犯罪・事故・災害などに関連して日々起こる重要な出来事をスピーディーかつ簡潔に読者に伝える内容となっている。新聞の読者、テレビやラジオの視聴者、さらにはインターネットの利用者にとって時間は最も貴重な資源であり、多くの人たちは限られた時間内に最大限の情報を入手する必要に迫られている。こうしたニーズに対応するために考案されたのが逆ピラミッド型と呼ばれるニュースの構成であり、Chapter 6 で紹介するフィーチャー・ニュース（feature news）の構成と対比される。

このトピックを英文で読んでみよう。

This news writing format summarizes the most important facts at the very start of the story. It may seem like an obvious idea to us nowadays—getting right to the point when you start a story—but it did not occur to most reporters until midway through the 19th century. What changed? Sentences got shorter. Writing got tighter. And reporters developed a formula for compressing the most newsworthy facts—the who, what, when, where, why—into the opening paragraphs of a story. That formula lives on today. It is known as the inverted pyramid.

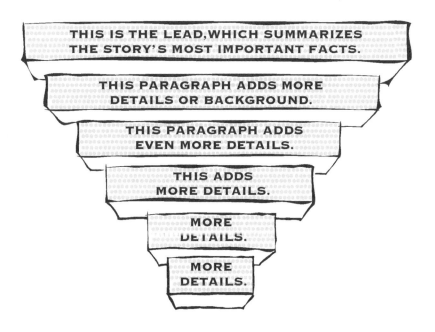

THIS IS THE LEAD, WHICH SUMMARIZES THE STORY'S MOST IMPORTANT FACTS.

THIS PARAGRAPH ADDS MORE DETAILS OR BACKGROUND.

THIS PARAGRAPH ADDS EVEN MORE DETAILS.

THIS ADDS MORE DETAILS.

MORE DETAILS.

MORE DETAILS.

NEWS 4

US formally starts withdrawal from WHO

The White House has formally notified the United Nations that it is pulling the United States out of the World Health Organization, despite the surging number of COVID-19 cases in the country.

President Donald Trump froze US funding for the WHO in April and a month later announced his intentions to drop out. He accused the organization of having a pro-China bias in its handling of the coronavirus outbreak and demanded reforms. 5

"We have detailed the reforms that it must make and engaged with them directly, but they have refused to act. Because they have failed to make the requested and greatly needed reforms, we will be today terminating the relationship," Trump said in May. 10

Under WHO rules, any country leaving the organization must give one year's notice. If Trump loses the November election, the next president could decide to remain.

Presumptive Democratic presidential nominee Joe Biden said if he is elected in November, he will rejoin the WHO "on my first day as president … and restore 15 our leadership on the world stage." Americans are safer when America is engaged in

strengthening global health, Biden said.

But Trump and other conservative critics of the WHO accuse the organization of spreading what they say was Chinese misinformation about the coronavirus early in the pandemic, including allegations that China deliberately tried to downplay the 20 dangers of the coronavirus and how it can spread through human-to-human contact.

US health experts call the president's decision to turn his back on the WHO shortsighted and destructive of decades of cooperation in fighting all diseases.

Democratic Speaker of the House Nancy Pelosi condemned Trump's decision as one of "true senselessness," she tweeted. "With millions of lives at risk, the president 25 is crippling the international effort to defeat the virus."

The United States is a charter member of the WHO, which was founded in 1948, and has been its biggest donor.

— Based on a report on VOANews.com on July 8, 2020 —

〈ニュース解説〉　世界各地で猛威をふるう新型コロナウイルス。これに立ち向かう国際的な連携を
リードすべき WHO（世界保健機関）が、感染防止に必要な情報を提供しなかったことが世界的蔓
延をもたらしたとして、トランプ米大統領は非難を強めた。同機関のテドロス事務局長が、出身国
エチオピアとの関係から、感染源とされる中国に配慮し、事態を過少評価したことが原因だとし、
2020 年 4 月、WHO への資金拠出を停止。翌 5 月、WHO 脱退の意向を表明し、7 月 8 日、正式
に国連に通告した。米国では、このニュースの時点で COVID-19 の症例数が世界で最も多い 300
万人を数え、131,000 人が死亡している。大統領選への思惑も交え、混乱は拡大の様相を見せた。

(Notes)

◆　**US formally starts withdrawal from WHO**　「米国　WHO 正式脱退へ」［″withdrawal″ は 脱退、撤退
　　の意。″WHO（World Health Organization：世界保健機関）″ は国連の専門機関として 1948 年
　　にジュネーブに設立。天然痘の撲滅など途上国の保健環境の向上や感染症の拡大を抑止する活
　　動を行ってきた］

◆ (L. 1)　**White House**　ホワイトハウス（当局）［″White House″ はアメリカ合衆国大統領官邸。ここ
　　では、「大統領行政府（the Executive Office of the President of the United States）」を指す。］

◆ (L. 1)　**United Nations** 国際連合（脱退通告は、WHO の上部組織である国連に対して行われた）

◆ (L. 1-2)　**pull ... out of 〜**　〜から…を引かせる（脱退させる）

◆ (L. 2-3)　**surging number of COVID-19 cases**　新型コロナウイルスの感染（者）数の急増

◆ (L. 4)　**US funding**　米国の資金拠出（米国は WHO に対する全拠出金の 15.18%を負担する最大拠出
　　国。ビル＆メリンダ・ゲイツ財団、英国、ドイツ、世界銀行等と続き、日本は EU に次いで、
　　国としては 5 番目となる 2.59%を拠出している。中国は国としては 23 番目の 0.21%だった）

◆ (L. 5)　**drop out**　脱退する

◆ (L. 6)　**pro-China bias**　中国寄りのバイアス（このほか、中国の反対により台湾を総会オブザーバー
　　として呼ばないなど中国におもねる姿勢を続けたとされる）

◆ (L. 6)　**reforms**　（WHO の）改革

◆ (L. 7)　**engaged with them directly**　WHO 事務当局と直接交渉した（″engage with″ は「〜と交戦
　　する」の意。ここでは「交渉する」）

◆ (L. 9)　**terminating the relationship**　関係を終了させる

◆ (L. 11-12)　**one year's notice**　1 年前の事前通告

◆ (L. 12-13)　**the next president could decide to remain**　次期大統領が残留を決断することは可能だ

◆ (L. 14)　**Presumptive Democratic presidential nominee Joe Biden**　（現時点で）民主党の大統領
　　候補になることが確実視されているジョー・バイデン氏（前オバマ政権の副大統領で中国と融
　　和的と見られていた）

◆ (L. 15)　**on my first day as president**　大統領に就任したその日に

◆ (L. 19)　**Chinese misinformation**　中国からの誤った情報

◆ (L. 20)　**allegations**　疑惑

◆ (L. 20)　**deliberately**　意図的に

◆ (L. 21)　**spread through human-to-human contact**　人から人への接触を通して感染が拡大する（当
　　初 WHO は、中国からの情報に基づき、「人―人感染」は確認されないと発表した）

◆ (L. 22)　**turn his back on**　〜に背を向ける

◆ (L. 24)　**Democratic Speaker of the House Nancy Pelosi**　民主党のナンシー・ペロシ下院議長

◆ (L. 25)　**"true senselessness"**　「まことに愚かな」

◆ (L. 26)　**cripple**　根底から覆す、ぶち壊しにする

◆ (L. 27)　**charter member**　創立メンバー

◆ (L. 28)　**biggest donor**　最大の資金拠出者

1. 本文の内容と一致するものには T (True) を、一致しないものには F (False) を記せ。

(　　　) (1) The United States has notified the United Nations of its formal intention to withdraw from the World Health Organization, although the country faces a surging number of the coronavirus infections.

(　　　) (2) President Donald Trump announced the country's intention to drop out of the WHO, then the US froze its funding for the organization.

(　　　) (3) Under the rules, any member country leaving the WHO must give the organization one year's notice.

(　　　) (4) Democratic presidential nominee Joe Biden said he will reconsider the pros and cons of the withdrawal from the WHO if he is elected in November.

(　　　) (5) Mr Trump accused the WHO of spreading so-called Chinese misinformation on the coronavirus early in the pandemic.

(　　　) (6) US Democratic leaders severely criticized President Trump's decision on the withdrawal from the WHO because the move could risk millions of lives and paralyze the international effort to defeat the virus.

(　　　) (7) The United States is one of the founding members of the WHO but has handed over the position of being its biggest financial contributor to China.

2. 米国の WHO 正式脱退通知は 2020 年 7 月 8 日に行われた。これを踏まえると、次の英文を完成させるため、下線部に入るべき文の選択肢 (a) ～ (d) のうち、論理的に適切でないものはどれか。

　　The United States will stay with the World Health Organization as a member country until ＿＿＿＿

　　(a) the presidential election day, November 3, 2020.

　　(b) New Year's Day, January 1, 2021.

　　(c) the eve of the presidential inauguration, January 19, 2021.

　　(d) the first anniversary of notification of withdrawal, July 8, 2021.

Natural
22

Slow
24

President Donald Trump said Saturday that he will postpone until the fall the meeting of the Group of 7 nations he had planned to hold next month at the White House despite the ongoing coronavirus pandemic. And he said he plans to invite Russia, Australia, South Korea and India as he again [(1)] _____ .

Trump told reporters that he feels the current makeup of the group is "very outdated" and doesn't properly represent "what's going on in the world." A White House official said that Trump wanted to bring in [(2)] _____ and those impacted by the coronavirus to discuss the future of China.

Natural
23

Slow
25

The surprise announcement came after German Chancellor Angela Merkel's office said Saturday that she would not attend the meeting unless [(3)] _____ had changed by then.

Trump announced in March he was canceling the summit because of the pandemic and that the leaders would confer by video conference instead. But Trump then switched course, saying a week ago that he was again [(4)] _____ .

Russia had been invited to attend the gathering of the world's most advanced economies since 1997, but was suspended in 2014 following its [(5)] _____ .

— *Based on a report on AP News.com on May 31, 2020* —

〈ニュース解説〉 2020 年の主要先進 7 か国首脳会議（G7 サミット）は、同年 3 月、議長国である米国が主催することとなっていたが、折からのコロナウイルス感染爆発を受け、6 月に延期された。だが、その開催が迫る中、コロナはますます猛威を振るうことになり、トランプ大統領は会議を再度延期し、9 月に対面で行うとともに、ロシアなど 4 か国を追加で招待する考えを明らかにした。1975 年、東西冷戦下の西側自由民主主義先進国の連帯の場として始まった G7 の根幹を揺るがす提案に、既存メンバーからの疑問が投げかけられることとなった。

(Notes)
meeting of the Group of 7 nations 主要先進 7 か国首脳会議（G7 サミット） **Russia, Australia, South Korea and India** ロシア、豪州、韓国及びインド（2014 年に G8 から脱落したロシアの再参加はトランプ大統領の持論。他の 3 国は対中政策での協力の観点から） **the current makeup of the group** 現在の G7 参加国の構成 **outdated** 時代遅れ **"what's going on in the world"**「世界の現状」 **the future of China** 今後の中国にどう対処するか **German Chancellor Angela Merkel** アンゲラ・メルケル独首相（"chancellor" はドイツやオーストリアの首相に用いられる） **video conference** テレビ（ビデオ）会議 **the gathering of the world's most advanced economies** 世界で最も先進的な経済（国家）の集まり（である首脳会議）（G7 サミットを指す。"economy" は経済の観点から見た「国」を表す）

■問A　空所 (a) ～ (f) にそれぞれ入るべき1語を下記の語群から選びその番号を記せ。

国連総会（UNGA）	→	United Nations General (a)
国連安全保障理事会（UNSC）	→	United Nations Security (b)
国連難民高等弁務官（UNHCR）	→	United Nations High (c) for Refugees
国連食糧農業機関（FAO）	→	(United Nations) Food and Agriculture (d)
国際原子力機関（IAEA）	→	International Atomic Energy (e)
国際通貨基金（IMF）	→	International Monetary (f)

> 1. Agency　　2. Assembly　　3. Commissioner　　4. Council
> 5. Forum　　6. Fund　　7. Operation　　8. Organization

■問B　(a) ～ (k) にそれぞれ入るべき1語を下記の語群から選びその番号を記せ。

国連教育科学文化機関（UNESCO）	→	United Nations (a), Scientific and Cultural Organization
国際労働機関（ILO）	→	International (b) Organization
世界保健機関（WHO）	→	World (c) Organization
世界貿易機関（WTO）	→	World (d) Organization
国際復興開発銀行（IBRD）	→	International Bank for (e) and Development
アジア太平洋経済協力（APEC）	→	Asia-Pacific (f) Cooperation
東南アジア諸国連合（ASEAN）	→	(g) of Southeast Asian Nations
北大西洋条約機構（NATO）	→	North Atlantic (h) Organization
石油輸出国機構（OPEC）	→	Organization of the (i) Exporting Countries
経済協力開発機構（OECD）	→	Organisation for Economic (j) and Development
国際エネルギー機関（IEA）	→	International (k) Agency

> 1. Association　　2. Co-operation　　3. Countries　　4. Economic
> 5. Educational　　6. Energy　　7. Healing　　8. Health
> 9. Labor　　10. Leaders　　11. Petroleum　　12. Power
> 13. Reconstruction　　14. Rehabilitation　　15. Trade　　16. Treaty

■問C　(a) ～ (g) をそれぞれ和訳せよ。

(a) Ambassador Extraordinary and Plenipotentiary
(b) diplomatic immunity
(c) ratification
(d) sovereignty
(e) COP
(f) exile
(g) economic sanctions

The lead — リードの役割

すべてのニュースがこの形をとるわけではないが、特に "hard news" は、リードと呼ばれる導入部でニュースの要約を伝えるのが普通である。一般に five W's and one H のすべての要素が、最初の 1 〜 2 の段落に凝縮される。「lead（リード）」は「headline（見出し）」のすぐ後に書かれ、リードの後に続くのが「body（本文）」である。ヘッドラインはスペース上の問題もあり記事の内容を正確に伝えきれないこともあるが、リードは記事の内容を冒頭で要約して、読者に端的に伝える。

このトピックを英文で読んでみよう。

A news story has two main parts: a lead and a body.

Usually the lead is the opening paragraph but may include the second and third paragraphs as well. It is the essence of the news as presented in summary form at the beginning of the story.

A typical lead is:

Telephone wires leading into 15 dwellings were cut yesterday afternoon, apparently by vandals, interrupting service for 25 users.

Leads have many constructions and patterns of their own. Generally, however, they seek to answer six questions about the news—Who? What? When? Where? Why? and How?

The body of the story is all the rest beyond the lead, no matter whether the remainder is three or 30 paragraphs long. The arrangement of the body often follows logically from the lead, but it, too, must be planned.

Suspect, Charged, Said to Admit to Role in Plot

FBI search a house where Faisal Shahzad lived in Bridgeport, Conn., Tuesday, May 4, 2010.

Chapter 5　軍事

NEWS 5

Chinese state media claims country's navy is not affected by coronavirus

Hong Kong—The coronavirus outbreak, which began in the Chinese city of Wuhan in December last year, has spread to more than 180 countries and sickened close to 2 million people, including more than 80,000 in China. Yet according to the Chinese government, not a single serving member of the country's military has been infected.   5

The reported absence of cases among China's armed forces comes despite the fact that thousands of military personnel were sent to Wuhan to assist in front line medical efforts. It also comes in sharp contrast to other military powers, notably the United States, which have seen an uptick in cases in recent weeks.

Earlier this week, a report detailing the deployment of a Chinese naval flotilla to 10
the Pacific was offered as evidence that the People's Liberation Army (PLA) Navy has reportedly done a better job controlling coronavirus than the US Navy. According to the report, which was first carried in the state-run tabloid Global Times, the aircraft carrier Liaoning led the group, which included two guided-missile destroyers, two guided-missile frigates and an auxiliary ship.   15

On the other hand, the USS Theodore Roosevelt, now docked in Guam, has been hit the hardest by the virus, with 589 positive cases among its crew of more than 4,000 people, as of Monday. Almost all of them have been moved ashore on the island, and work is going on to disinfect the ship, delaying its ability to deploy.

Under Chinese President Xi Jinping, the PLA has modernized its forces in an 20
effort to be among the world's strongest and most capable. It also has worked hard to project an image both at home and abroad of a military superpower equal to the US.

US observers, however, have cast doubt on the PLA's claims that its naval operations have not been impacted by the virus. Carl Schuster, a former Navy captain and Hawaii Pacific University instructor, said the PLA was able to mask any effects 25
because its ships operate close to Chinese shores, meaning time at sea is limited. "Short deployments of under 20 days will preclude the disease affecting operations during the so-called deployment and pulling into a military base all but precludes any evidence of an outbreak becoming public knowledge," Schuster said.

The Western Pacific has become an area of potential confrontation between the 30
US and Chinese navies in recent years, with the South China Sea a particular thorn in bilateral relations. China claims almost the entire 1.3 million square mile South China Sea as its sovereign territory, and it has aggressively asserted its stake in recent years in the face of conflicting claims from several Southeast Asian nations.

— Based on a report on CNN.com on April 15, 2020 —

〈ニュース解説〉　新型コロナウィルスの感染が拡大する中、アメリカ海軍空母「セオドア・ルーズベルト」の艦内でも感染者が出たため、しばらくグアム島の海軍基地に係留されることとなった。他にも数隻の空母でコロナ感染者が見つかり作戦展開能力が低下した米海軍に対し、その真偽はともかく中国艦船での感染者ゼロを自賛する中国人民解放軍海軍は、米海軍艦船不在の隙をついて空母「遼寧」を沖縄本島と宮古島間の海域を南下させ、台湾東部から南部に威嚇航行させている。本文では、感染者ゼロのからくりと、西太平洋や南シナ海での米中海軍の対峙に言及がされている。

(Notes)

◆ **state media**　国営メディア［state-run media のこと。中国政府が管理するため中国共産党の意向が強く反映される。人民日報（People's Daily）、新華社（Xinhua シンホワと発音、或いは New China News Agency とも称される）、後述の環球時報（2009 年にその英語版 Global Times が創刊）等がある］

◆ (L. 1)　**coronavirus outbreak**　コロナウィルスの集団感染

◆ (L. 2)　**Wuhan**　武漢［新型コロナウイルス感染症（世界保健機関 WHO の正式呼称は COVID-19）については、生きた動物や魚介類を扱う武漢華南海鮮卸売市場との関連が指摘されたり、武漢ウイルス研究所からウイルスが漏洩した可能性の指摘もあり、トランプ米大統領等は "Wuhan Virus" と呼び続けた］

◆ (L. 9)　**uptick**　（数量等の）上昇、増加

◆ (L. 10)　**flotilla**　小艦隊

◆ (L. 11)　**People's Liberation Army Navy**　（中国）人民解放軍海軍［人民解放軍は中国共産党の軍事組織で国軍に相当する。かつては中国沿岸部の防衛が主たる任務であったが、最近は第 1 列島線（九州から沖縄、台湾、フィリピン、ボルネオ島に至るライン）を超えて第 2 列島線（伊豆諸島から小笠原諸島、グアム、サイパン、パプアニューギニアに至るライン）までの制海権を握ろうとし、最終的には西太平洋全域に影響力を及ぼそうと計画している］

◆ (L. 12)　**US Navy**　米国海軍［米軍（United States Armed Forces）は、Chapter 5 の VOCABULARY BUILDUP 問 B にある 4 軍の他に、宇宙軍（Space Force）、沿岸警備隊（Coast Guard）を入れる場合がある］

◆ (L. 13-14)　**state-run tabloid Global Times**　国営タブロイド紙の環球時報［中国共産党機関紙の人民日報系列紙であり、Web news も提供している。タブロイド判は、285mm×400mm の小型の新聞で、英国では、The Sun や労働党支持の The Daily Mirror 等の大衆紙がある。これより大きい判としては、ベルリーナ判（315mm×470mm）や普通サイズ（大判紙、375mm×600mm）のブロードシート判がある。日本の一般紙は、これと比べると左右の寸法に若干の違いがある］

◆ (L. 14)　**aircraft carrier Liaoning**　（中国の）航空母艦「遼寧」（日本語で「りょうねい」、中国語で「リャオニン」と読む。旧ソ連が設計しウクライナ所有であった未完成空母「ヴァリャーグ」を中国が購入して中国初の空母に改修。中国は 2019 年末に、国産初の空母「山東（シャントン）」を就役させている）

◆ (L. 14-15)　**guided-missile destroyer**　（誘導）ミサイル駆逐艦

◆ (L. 15)　**guided-missile frigates**　（誘導）ミサイル・フリゲート艦（フリゲート艦は時代や国によってその基準がはっきりしなく曖昧であるが、ここでは駆逐艦より小型の艦船を指す）

◆ (L. 15)　**auxiliary ship**　補助艦船（戦闘用艦艇ではないが、補給、給油、輸送等艦隊の洋上展開において重要な役割を演じる）

◆ (L. 16)　**USS Theodore Roosevelt**　米国海軍艦船「セオドア・ルーズベルト」［米国第 26 代大統領にちなんで命名された航空母艦。USS は United States Ship の略で、米国海軍艦船につけられる艦船接頭辞。JS は Japan Ship の略で、海上自衛隊艦船の外国名に付けられ、英国海軍艦船には HMS（Her 又は His Majesty's Ship）の艦船接頭辞が付く］

◆ (L. 17)　**positive case**　陽性症例

◆ (L. 20)　**Chinese President Xi Jinping**　習近平中国国家主席（発音はシージンピン）

◆ (L. 24)　**Carl Schuster**　カール・シュスター（退役海軍大佐で、米太平洋軍統合情報センター前作戦部長であった。2000 年以降ハワイ・パシフィック大学で教鞭をとる）

◆ (L. 28)　**all but**　ほとんど、〜も同然で（almost）

◆ (L. 32-33)　**almost the entire 1.3 million square mile South China Sea**　130 万平方マイルの広さを持つ南シナ海のほぼ全域

1. 本文の内容と一致するものには T (True) を、一致しないものには F (False) を記せ。

(　　　) (1) The article denies any deaths among coronavirus infected people outside Wuhan at the time of writing.

(　　　) (2) Globally, the majority of coronavirus patients are Chinese people living outside China.

(　　　) (3) The article seems to be 100 percent behind the Chinese government's insistence that their military is entirely free from coronavirus infection.

(　　　) (4) Having allegedly controlled the spread of coronavirus, the Chinese Navy seems to stand in a better position than the US Navy to deploy the naval vessels to the Pacific.

(　　　) (5) It can safely be surmised that the state-run paper Global Times can report both favorable and unfavorable news about the Chinese government.

(　　　) (6) After quickly and successfully handling coronavirus outbreak, the aircraft carrier USS Theodore Roosevelt was deployed to the Pacific to exercise vigilance against Chinese naval activities.

(　　　) (7) More than half the crew of the USS Theodore Roosevelt turned up positive in the coronavirus tests.

(　　　) (8) Chinese President Xi Jinping is trying to give the impression that his military is on a par with the United States armed forces.

(　　　) (9) A former US navy captain opines that the reported absence of coronavirus infection among Chinese servicemen is doubtful, as the Chinese navy can easily hide the evidence of an outbreak due to its ships' proximity to their base along with their short-term deployments of less than three weeks.

2. 次の英文を完成させるために、(a) 〜 (d) から最も適切なものを１つ選べ。

There is a fear of a possible showdown between the US and Chinese navies in the wake of _____

(a) China's assertiveness in the South China Sea.

(b) China's abandonment of its sovereign status in the South China Sea islands.

(c) the establishment of friendly relationships between the US and several Southeast Asian nations in an attempt to isolate China.

(d) the sudden deployment of the US naval vessels in the Western Pacific.

音声を聞き、下線部を補え。（２回録音されています。１回目はナチュラルスピード、２回目はスロースピードです。）

Natural 28
Slow 30

The Philippines has filed a diplomatic protest over China's creation of new districts [(1)] _____, Foreign Affairs Secretary Teodoro Locsin Jr. said Wednesday. Aside from this, Locsin said that the Philippines also protested China's alleged pointing of a radar gun at a Philippine Navy ship in Philippine waters. "These are both [(2)] _____ _____," Locsin said.

China created two new districts of Sansha City, the southernmost city of Hainan province, which cover features in the disputed South China Sea, including the Philippine-claimed Spratly Islands, Scarborough Shoal and Fiery Cross Reef.

Natural 29
Slow 31

President Rodrigo Duterte [(3)] _____, despite its continued aggression in the West Philippine Sea, areas Manila claims and occupies in the South China Sea.

A 2016 ruling by a Hague-based arbitral tribunal backed by the Permanent Court of Arbitration [(4)] _____ over virtually the entire South China Sea based on so-called historical rights, but [(5)] _____.

— *Based on a report on CNN.com on April 22, 2020* —

5

10

15

〈ニュース解説〉　中国政府は 2020 年 4 月 20 日までに南シナ海に新行政区として「西沙区」及び「南沙区」を新設すると発表。これまで進めてきた南シナ海の環礁の埋め立てと軍事化による実効支配をさらに強化する姿勢を示した。「西沙区」にはパラセル諸島やスカボロー礁があり、「南沙区」にはスプラトリー諸島が含まれ、これまで周辺の東南アジア諸国や台湾と領有権をめぐる争いがあった。4 月初めには、中国海警局の艦船がベトナム漁船に体当たりして沈没させている。中国海警局は、日本の海上保安庁や諸外国の沿岸警備隊（Coast Guard）と異なり 2018 年に軍の指揮下に置かれている。

(Notes)

Foreign Affairs Secretary Teodoro Locsin Jr. テオドロ・ロクシン（フィリピン）外務大臣　**China's alleged pointing of a radar gun** 中国のレーダー照射疑惑（レーダー照射は、ミサイル等で攻撃標的にレーダーの照準を合わせる行為で、攻撃をなしうる状態にあることを示し、照射を受けた側は回避行動が必要となる）　**Sansha city** 三沙市（中国海南省の南東部に位置し、南シナ海の西沙、中沙、南沙諸島を管轄する）　**features** 地勢、地形、地（e.g. disputed features 係争地）　**Hainan Province** 海南省（海南島と周りの島嶼部からなる。省都は海口市）　**the Philippine-claimed Spratly Islands, Scarborough Shoal and Fiery Cross Reef** フィリピンが領有を主張するスプラトリー諸島、スカボロー礁及びファイアリー・クロス礁　**President Rodrigo Duterte** ロドリゴ・ドゥテルテ（フィリピン）大統領　**Manila** フィリピン或いはフィリピン政府　**Hague-based arbitral tribunal** ハーグに本拠を置く仲裁法廷（ハーグは、英語では The Hague ザ・ヘイグ、オランダ語では Den Haag デン・ハーフと呼ばれる）　**Permanent Court of Arbitration** 常設仲裁裁判所

■問A 自衛隊関連用語 (a) 〜 (d) にそれぞれ入るべき１語を下記の語群から選びその番号を記せ。

自衛隊　　　　→　Japan Self-Defense (a)
陸上自衛隊　　→　Japan (b) Self-Defense Force
海上自衛隊　　→　Japan (c) Self-Defense Force
航空自衛隊　　→　Japan (d) Self-Defense Force

1. Air　　2. Force　　3. Forces　　4. Ground　　5. Maritime　　6. Sea

■問B 米軍関連用語 (a) 〜 (e) をそれぞれ和訳せよ。

(a) United States Armed Forces
(b) United States Army
(c) United States Navy
(d) United States Air Force
(e) United States Marine Corps

■問C 軍事用語 (a) 〜 (d) をそれぞれ和訳せよ。

(a) anti-ballistic missile (ABM)
(b) airborne warning and control system (AWACS)
(c) intermediate-range ballistic missile (IRBM)［射程距離の短い準中距離弾道ミサイルは、medium-range ballistic missile（MRBM）と呼ばれるが、IRBM との区別は明確ではない］
(d) Nuclear Non-Proliferation Treaty (NPT)

■問D (a) 〜 (j) にそれぞれ対応する英語表現を下記の語群から選びその番号を記せ。

(a) 平和維持活動　　(b) 非武装地帯　　(c) 文民統制　　(d) 核軍縮
(e) 核保有国　　(f) 通常兵器　　(g) 地雷　　(h) 休戦
(i) 大量破壊兵器　　(j) 自爆テロ

1. ceasefire　　2. civilian control
3. conventional weapons　　4. demilitarized zone (DMZ)
5. landmine　　6. nuclear disarmament
7. nuclear powers　　8. peacekeeping operations
9. terrorist suicide bombing　　10. weapons of mass destruction (WMD)

Beyond the basic news lead ― 異なるスタイルのリード

社会問題や面白そうな人物を扱った記事等、解説的要素が大きく入り込む記事においては、前章で触れたような事実だけを並べた要約的なリードで記事を書き始めたのでは何とも味気ない。すべてのニュースが時宜を得たものであるとは限らない。昨日今日のニュースのように即時性が要求されるニュースでない場合は、もっと生き生きしたクリエイティヴで掘り下げた、場合によっては楽しく人をわくわくさせる記事の書き方が求められる。

このトピックを英文で読んでみよう。

It is not mandatory to begin every story with a roundup of essential facts. For most breaking news events, you need leads that are quick, factual, and concise. You need leads that summarize the who-what-when-where-why. But not every story is a timely news event. Some stories explore social issues. Some profile interesting people. And for those, a basic news lead may be too dull and dry. You may need something livelier, snappier, more creative, a lead that does not just summarize, but amuses, astonishes, and intrigues.

NEWS MEDIA IN THE WORLD

通信社　News Agencies (1)

✓ "news agency" や "news service" と呼ばれる「通信社」は、独自の取材陣又は国内外の報道機関などと連携し、作成したニュース記事を写真やビデオ映像などとともに新聞社、放送会社へ配信する組織。膨大な取材ネットワークが必要なため、単独の新聞社等では対応が困難なことから、報道機関が共同して通信社を設ける非営利型の組合組織も多い。

NEWS 6

Disk 1
32

Trump administration sues to delay release of Bolton book

The Trump administration sued former national security adviser John Bolton on Tuesday to delay the publication of a book that the White House says contains classified information and that is expected to paint an unfavorable portrait of the president's foreign policy decision-making.

The civil lawsuit in Washington's federal court follows warnings from President 5 Donald Trump that Bolton could face a "criminal problem" if he doesn't halt plans to publish the book, which is scheduled for release next week.

The complaint is the latest salvo in a contentious relationship between Trump and the hawkish Bolton, who was abruptly forced from the White House last September after repeated disagreements on national security matters. It moves their 10 rift into court, where a judge will be asked to decide whether Bolton short-circuited proper procedures to get his book on the marke—something his lawyer and publisher have strongly denied.

In its lawsuit, the Justice Department administration contends that the former adviser did not complete a pre-publication review to ensure that the manuscript did 15 not contain classified material.

33 Bolton's book, "The Room Where It Happened: A White House Memoir," was supposed to be released in March. Its release date was twice delayed and it is now set to be released next week by Simon & Schuster.

"Bolton covers an array of topics—chaos in the White House, sure, but also 20 assessments of major players, the president's inconsistent, scattershot decision-making process, and his dealings with allies and enemies alike, from China, Russia, Ukraine, North Korea, Iran, the United Kingdom, France, and Germany," according to the publisher.

The book has been highly anticipated for months, especially after news broke 25 during Trump's impeachment trial that the manuscript offered a vivid account of the president's efforts to freeze military aid to Ukraine until the country assisted with investigations into Trump's political rival Joe Biden. Those allegations formed the crux of the impeachment case, which ended in February with the president's acquittal in the Senate.

— Based on an AP report on VOANews.com on June 17, 2020 —

〈ニュース解説〉 2020年11月に実施される米国大統領選挙。再選を目指すトランプ氏の行く手を遮ったのは、トランプ氏が更迭したジョン・ボルトン前大統領補佐官だ。超タカ派の姿勢を貫くボルトン氏と場当たり的に「取引」を重視して対外政策を進めるトランプ氏との溝は深まり、ボルトン氏は政権を去る。その一年半の経験をもとに、トランプ氏の真実を著書にまとめたという。政権は、同書の内容が大統領選に影響することをおそれ、その出版延期を裁判所に求めた。

(Notes)

◆ **Trump administration sues to delay release of Bolton book**　「トランプ政権　ボルトン氏著書の出版延期求め提訴」（"administration" は「政権」。"sue" は「訴える」「提訴する」。"delay" は他動詞で「遅らせる」。"Bolton book" はボルトン前大統領補佐官が著した「暴露本」を指す。トランプ政権は、同氏が著作中の国家機密の有無を確認する手続きに違反しているとして出版延期を求め、連邦地裁に提訴した）

◆ (L. 1)　**former national security adviser John Bolton**　ジョン・ボルトン前国家安全保障担当大統領補佐官（ボルトン氏は名門イェール大学ロースクールを卒業し、弁護士、司法省勤務等を経て、ジョージ・W・ブッシュ政権の国務次官、駐国連大使を務めた。強硬な保守派として知られ、2018年4月からトランプ大統領の補佐官として北朝鮮やイラン、中国などを含む安全保障問題を担当。トランプ氏と政策上の意見が相違し、2019年9月辞任した。肩書にある "former" は「前」「元」両方を含む概念だが、本ニュース時点では「前」だった）

◆ (L. 3)　**classified information**　機密情報（後出の "classified material" も同義。国家機密を扱う公務員は、機密事項については、辞職後も口外を禁じられる罰則付きの守秘義務がある）

◆ (L. 3)　**paint an unfavorable portrait of**　好ましからぬ姿を描く

◆ (L. 4)　**foreign policy decision-making**　外交政策決定

◆ (L. 5)　**civil lawsuit**　民事訴訟（犯罪行為が明白でないため、まず民事訴訟に訴えた）

◆ (L. 5)　**Washington's federal court**　ワシントンの連邦（地方）裁判所

◆ (L. 6)　**"criminal problem"**　「刑事訴追問題」（守秘義務違反として罰せられる可能性を意味する）

◆ (L. 8)　**complaint**　提訴（民事訴訟において訴を提起すること）

◆ (L. 8)　**latest salvo in a contentious relationship**　衝突を繰り返してきた両者間の最新の争い

◆ (L. 9)　**hawkish Bolton**　タカ派のボルトン氏

◆ (L. 10-11)　**It moves their rift into court**　提訴によって両者の不和が法廷に持ち込まれた

◆ (L. 11-12)　**short-circuited proper procedures**　適切な手続きを省いた（機密情報の精査を短期間で済まそうとした）

◆ (L. 14)　**Justice Department administration**　司法省当局

◆ (L. 15)　**pre-publication review**　出版前査閲

◆ (L. 17)　**"The Room Where It Happened: A White House Memoir"**　[直訳すれば「それが起きた部屋：ホワイトハウス回想録」。"the room" は「大統領執務室（楕円形をしていることから "Oval Room" と呼ばれる）」を指すと考えられる]

◆ (L. 19)　**Simon & Schuster**　サイモン＆シュースター社（1924年創業の出版最大手。本社、NY）

◆ (L. 21)　**inconsistent, scattershot**　一貫性なく闇雲な ["scattershot" は「散弾（の発射）」か原義]

◆ (L. 26)　**Trump's impeachment trial**　トランプ大統領の弾劾裁判（「職権乱用」と「議会妨害」で起訴された）

◆ (L. 26)　**vivid account of**　〜に関する生々しい描写

◆ (L. 27-28)　**freeze military aid to Ukraine ... Trump's political rival Joe Biden**　（ウクライナに対し、大統領選対抗馬のジョー・バイデン氏への疑惑捜査を迫り、軍事援助を凍結したことを指す）

◆ (L. 29-30)　**acquittal in the Senate**　上院での無罪（判決）（2020年2月5日無罪となっていた）

1. 本文の内容と一致するものには T (True) を、一致しないものには F (False) を記せ。

(　) (1) The US government took legal action against former national security adviser John Bolton, demanding him to postpone the release of his new book so as to avoid possible damage to President Donald Trump.

(　) (2) After the civil lawsuit commenced in Washington's federal court, the White House warned Bolton that he could face a "criminal problem" if he failed to halt his plans to publish the book.

(　) (3) Bolton was suddenly forced to leave his job last September after repeated disagreements with Trump on national security matters.

(　) (4) The Justice Department claims that Mr Bolton did not complete a pre-publication review to ensure that his book contained classified material.

(　) (5) The crux of Trump's impeachment case was made up of allegations that the president had tried to freeze military aid to Ukraine until the country assisted with investigations into Trump's rival Joe Biden.

(　) (6) Trump's impeachment process ended with the president's acquittal in the Senate after the release of the Bolton's book.

2. 次の英文を完成させるために、(a) ～ (d) から最も適切なものを１つ選べ。

According to the publisher, Bolton's book covers chaos in the White House, three of the topics below, but not _____

(a) the president's inconsistent, scattershot decision–making process.

(b) mistakes made by the author himself.

(c) the president's dealings with allies and enemies.

(d) assessments of major players.

音声を聞き、下線部を補え。（２回録音されています。１回目はナチュラルスピード、２回目はスロースピードです。）

Natural
34
Slow
36

HONG KONG—Prominent Hong Kong democracy activist Nathan Law has left the city for an undisclosed location after testifying in a US congressional hearing about the tough new security law imposed by mainland China [(1)] _____ .

Law, who declined to disclose his whereabouts for safety, said in an interview with the Associated Press on Friday that he left because Hong Kong needs [(2)] _____ internationally.   5

Under the new security law, activists and politicians in Hong Kong who speak to foreign media or testify in foreign hearings can be arrested for secessionism or colluding with foreign forces, Law said.   10

Natural
35
Slow
37

The security law, [(3)] _____ , targets secessionist, subversive or terrorist acts, as well as collusion with foreign forces intervening in the city's affairs.

Under Beijing's direction, local authorities have moved swiftly to implement the law's sweeping conditions, with police arresting about 370 people Wednesday, including 10 on suspicion of directly violating the law, as thousands [(4)] _____ .   15

Critics, including Law, say the legislation effectively ends the "one country, two systems" framework under which the city was promised [(5)] _____ when it reverted from British to Chinese rule in 1997.   20

— *Based on an AP report on VOANews.com on July 3, 2020* —

〈ニュース解説〉　香港立法会で上程された中国への犯罪者引き渡し条例案に反対する抗議デモは、香港全市民の３分の１が参加するまでに盛り上がった。世界の耳目が集まる中、中国政府は強硬手段に出ることを避け、同条例案は撤回された。だが、事態を見過ごせば、本土での民主化運動をも引き起こしかねないとの危機感から、2020 年 6 月 30 日、中国政府は香港国家安全維持法を制定し、香港での民主化運動を分離活動、外国勢力との共謀とみなし、厳格に取り締まる方針へ舵を切った。1997 年の中国復帰時、「中英共同声明」に基づき、香港の高度な自治は 50 年間維持されるとした「一国二制度」維持の国際公約は、23 年を経て、危機を迎えることとなった。

(Notes)
Hong Kong democracy activist 香港民主派の指導者　**Nathan Law** ネイサン・ロー（中国名；羅冠聡）　**US congressional hearing** 米国議会公聴会　**the city** 香港を指す　**undisclosed location** 非公開の行き先　**new security law** 香港国家安全維持法（略称「国安法」）　**mainland China** 中国本土（の政府）　**whereabouts** 居場所　**the Associated Press** AP 通信（米国の通信社：本ニュースの配信元）　**foreign media** 外国メディア　**secessionism or colluding with foreign forces** 分離活動又は外国勢力との共謀　**subversive or terrorist acts** 破壊活動又はテロ行為　**Beijing's direction**　中国政府の指示（"Beijing" は首都名で当該国や政府を指す用法）　**local authorities** 現地（香港）治安当局　**the law's sweeping conditions** 取締りの実施要件　**the "one country, two systems"**「一国二制度」　**it reverted from British to Chinese rule** 英国から中国に統治権が復帰した

■問A 米国政府関連用語 (a) 〜 (i) にそれぞれ入るべき1語を下記の語群から選びその番号を記せ。

司法省	→	Department of (a)
財務省	→	Department of the (b)
内務省	→	Department of the (c)
国防総省	→	Department of (d)
中央情報局	→	Central (e) Agency
国家安全保障会議	→	National (f) Council
連邦捜査局	→	Federal Bureau of (g)
米国通商代表部	→	Office of the United States (h) Representative
国土安全保障省	→	Department of (i) Security

1. Defense   2. Homeland   3. Intelligence   4. Interior   5. Investigation
6. Justice   7. Security   8. Trade   9. Treasury

■問B (a) 〜 (o) にそれぞれ対応する英文名称を下記の語群から選びその番号を記せ。

(a)（米）連邦議会　　(b)（米）下院　　(c)（米）上院
(d)（英）議会　　(e)（英）下院　　(f)（英）上院
(g)（米）民主党　　(h)（米）共和党　　(i)（英）自由民主党
(j)（英）労働党　　(k)（英）保守党　　(l)（米）国務長官
(m)（米）司法長官　　(n)（英）内相　　(o)（英）財務相（蔵相）

1. Attorney General
2. Chancellor of the Exchequer
3. Congress
4. Conservative Party
5. Democratic Party
6. Home Secretary
7. House of Commons
8. House of Lords
9. House of Representatives
10. Labour Party
11. Liberal Democratic Party
12. Parliament
13. Republican Party
14. Secretary of State
15. Senate

■問C (a) 〜 (e) のアジア関連用語をそれぞれ和訳せよ。

(a) National People's Congress

(b) People's Liberation Army

(c) People's Daily

(d) Republic of Korea (ROK)

(e) Democratic People's Republic of Korea (DPRK)

The world of features ― フィーチャー・ニュースの世界

"feature news"（フィーチャー・ニュース）は日本語では「特集記事」や「読み物」などと訳される。また、"hard news" と対比して "soft news" と呼ばれることもある。日本を台風が直撃し、その当日あるいは翌日、その被害を報じれば "hard news" である。その後、台風で家を失った住民の生活に焦点を当てて報じれば "feature news" となる。新聞などで報じられるニュースの大半は "hard news" であるが、報道のスピードという点で新聞はインターネットに遅れを取らざるを得ず、インターネットの普及に伴い、新聞の記事に占める "feature news" の割合が増加傾向にあるとの指摘もある。

このトピックを英文で読んでみよう。

Some old-timers treat news and features as if they are two separate things. News, they insist, is the factual reporting of serious events, while features involve all that other, nonessential stuff. It is not that simple, though. Journalists often find it difficult to distinguish between news and features. News stories usually focus on events that are timely and public: government activity, crime, disasters. Feature stories often focus on issues that are less timely and more personal: trends, relationships, entertainment. News stories tell you what happened; feature stories offer you advice, explore ideas, and make you laugh and cry.

NEWS MEDIA IN THE WORLD

通信社　News Agencies (2)

✔　世界最初の近代的通信社は 1835 年フランスに生まれたアバスを母体とする AFP 通信（Agence France-Presse）。19 世紀半ばに創立の英国のロイター通信（Reuters）も業界の老舗。同時期に米国で設立された AP 通信（Associated Press）は組合型通信社の最大手。両社とも全世界に取材網を持ち、近時は経済ニュースにも力を入れる。経済情報の分野では Bloomberg の影響力も侮れない。

NEWS 7

Disk 1
38

Mental health impact grows amid restraint

As people are urged to practice self-restraint from nonessential trips outside their homes amid the new coronavirus outbreak, the number of those seeking advice on dealing with stress and other mental problems is on the rise in both the public and private sectors.

On social networking sites, such keywords as "corona stress" and "corona 5 depression" have become prevalent. Experts have advised measures for dealing with coronavirus-related stress, such as making a daily schedule and talking with others over the phone.

"Have I become neurotic about coronavirus? While I am not physically exhausted, I am exhausted mentally, so I cannot sleep well," said a 33-year-old 10 housewife from Soka, Saitama Prefecture, lamenting her loss of sleep on Twitter earlier this month.

She went on to say that because the kindergarten that her 5-year-old eldest son attends has been closed since about a month prior, they spend their time together during the day. Afraid of being infected, she cannot even take him out to the 15 neighborhood park, and they are almost completely at home.

As the sleepless nights continued, she became prone to raising her voice when her son behaved even a bit selfishly or made minor mistakes. Seeing on social media how merrily her "mom friends" appeared to be spending time together with their children, she would fall into a state of self-hatred, blaming herself, thinking, "Why 20 can't I raise my child properly?" As a result, exchanging messages with her "mom friends" became somewhat of a bother. It became clear to her that "I sometimes feel anxiety that I may not be fine."

The results of an analysis done by the Health, Labor and Welfare Ministry on 39 mental health consultations filed between Feb. 7 and the end of March at mental 25 health and welfare centers of local governments nationwide showed that about 1,700 of the cases were related to the new coronavirus. The matters discussed during the consultations were diverse. Some people fear being infected saying, "I am so frightened of being infected that I cannot go outdoors," or "The shortage of masks is causing me to panic." Others express concerns about their livelihoods, saying, "We 30 can't use caretaking facilities (for the elderly) and I got tired from caretaking."

Mariko Ukiyo, representative director of the Japanese Organization of Mental Health and Educational Agencies who also acts as an advisor, said, "As people practice self-restraint from leaving their homes, feelings of isolation sneak up on them, put them at risk of a 'coronavirus depression.' I recommend they create 35 opportunities to release stress by talking with friends over the phone, for instance."

Takashi Ebisawa, a 60-year-old psychiatrist and medical director of Rokubancho Mental Clinic in Chiyoda Ward, Tokyo, said, "Should mental stress that a person has no prior experience with continue to disrupt their lifestyle, they may develop symptoms including irregular sleep patterns and a lack of appetite. It is important to 40 control stress through activities such as regular exercise."

— Based on a report on The Japan News on April 27, 2020 —

〈ニュース解説〉　新型コロナウィルスの感染拡大が長期化するにつれて、心の不調を訴える人が増加。ウィルス感染や経済面での不安、外出自粛での閉塞感などが影響して心の落ち込み症状が深刻な人も多い。こうした状況を踏まえ、国や専門機関は相談窓口を開設し、メンタルケアに乗り出した。

(Notes)

◆ **(L. 5)　social networking site**　ソーシャルネットワーキングサイト（Facebook や Twitter などの交流サイト。略称 SNS）

◆ **(L. 5-6)　corona depression**　コロナ鬱（新型コロナウィルス感染拡大に伴い生じたさまざまな精神的不調を指す）

◆ **(L. 9)　become neurotic about**　〜に極度に神経質になる、神経過敏になる（ここでは、前段落の "corona stress"、"corona depression" などの症状を指す）

◆ **(L. 11)　Soka, Saitama Prefecture**　埼玉県草加市（埼玉県南東部に位置する人口 25 万人の市）

◆ **(L. 13)　go on to (do)**　次に〜する、続けて〜する

◆ **(L. 17)　prone to (doing)**　〜しがちである、〜しやすい

◆ **(L. 20)　self-hatred**　自己嫌悪

◆ **(L. 24)　Health, Labor and Welfare Ministry**　厚生労働省（正式名称は "Ministry of Health, Labour and Welfare" で Labour は英国式綴り）

◆ **(L. 25-26)　mental health and welfare center**　精神保健福祉センター（心の健康の保持と向上のため各都道府県に設置された支援機関。医師や臨床心理士などの専門家が精神保健福祉相談に対応しており、医療機関や支援機関についての情報提供なども行っている）

◆ **(L. 26)　local government**　地方自治体、地方公共団体

◆ **(L. 32-33)　Mariko Ukiyo, representative director of the Japanese Organization of Mental Health and Educational Agencies**　全国心理業連合会の浮世満理子代表理事（全国心理業連合会は一般社団法人の心理カウンセラー業界団体）

◆ **(L. 34)　sneak up on**　〜にこっそり近づく、忍び寄る

◆ **(L. 37)　Takashi Ebisawa**　海老澤尚

◆ **(L. 37-38)　Rokubancho Mental Clinic**　六番町メンタルクリニック

◆ **(L. 38)　Chiyoda Ward**　千代田区（"ward" は政令指定都市の行政区画としての「区」にあたる語。HP などでは "city" が用いられることも多い）

◆ **(L. 38-39)　Should mental stress that a person has no prior experience with continue to disrupt their lifestyle, ...**（"If mental stress that a person has no prior experience with should continue to disrupt their lifestyle,…" の条件節の if が省略されたことにより、should が文頭に来る倒置文となっている）

◆ **(L. 39-40)　develop symptoms**　発症する、症状が出る

ニュースを読んで、下記の設問に答えよ。

1. 本文の内容と一致するものには T (True) を、一致しないものには F (False) を記せ。

(   ) (1) The number of SNS posts that reflect growing fatigue among the public has increased, as people have refrained from going out.

(   ) (2) The 33-year-old mother of a 5-year-old son feels so much strain that she cannot stop exchanging messages with her friends.

(   ) (3) According to an analysis conducted by the Health, Labor and Welfare Ministry, many people face difficulty in dealing with their stress but are optimistic about their future.

(   ) (4) Mariko Ukiyo advises people to keep in touch with others via the phone and the like to ward off a sense of isolation.

(   ) (5) Dr. Takashi Ebisawa says unprecedented continuous stress may lead to health deterioration.

2. 下記の英文は、世界保健機関（WHO）が新型コロナウィルスの関連情報としてホームページで紹介したストレス対処法に関する記事の一部である。空所 (1) 及び (2) に入るべき適語をそれぞれ語群 (a) ～ (d) から選び記号で答えよ。

Limit worry and agitation by (1)_____ the time you and your family spend watching or listening to media coverage that you perceive as upsetting. Draw on skills you have used in the past that have helped you to manage life's previous (2)_____ and use those skills to help you manage your emotions during the challenging time of this outbreak.

(1) (a) killing   (b) lessening   (c) optimizing   (d) using

(2) (a) adversities   (b) discrepancies   (c) humiliations   (d) restrictions

音声を聞き、下線部を補え。（２回録音されています。１回目はナチュラルスピード、２回目はスロースピードです。）

Natural
40
Slow
42

The ruling Liberal Democratic Party's working group that is studying a move of the start of the school year to September is officially recommending against it, instead (1) _____ up to a month.

On June 2, members of the group handed Prime Minister Shinzo Abe their formal recommendation, (2) _____ for such a major shift.

Natural
41
Slow
43

"It is very difficult to introduce such change immediately, like in this fiscal year or the next fiscal year," the recommendation said. "Such broadly based institutional reform (3) _____ to form a public consensus and also to carry out."

The issue needs to be further discussed by "committees set up under the prime minister, and (4) _____,
while listening thoroughly to the voices of (5) _____
_____," it said.

5

10

15

— *Based on a report on asahi.com on June 2, 2020* —

〈ニュース解説〉 新型コロナウィルスの影響で長期休校措置が続いたことにより浮上した「9月入学」制度の導入は、社会に及ぼす混乱の大きさや種々の問題点が指摘され見送られることになった。コロナ対策で巨額の財政支出が求められ、学校も感染対策に忙殺されている現状では、現在の社会の仕組みを根底から変えるような変革をすべきではないとの声が高まった。9月入学には利点も多いため、長期的に課題を精査したうえでの制度導入には検討の余地を残している。

(Notes)
recommend against 〜を勧めない　**institutional reform** 制度改革　**related ministries and agencies**
関係省庁

VOCABULARY BUILDUP

■問A　空所 (a) ～ (j) にそれぞれ入るべき1語を下記の語群から選びその番号を記せ。

体罰	→	(a) punishment
帰国子女	→	(b) children
ひきこもり	→	social (c)
ネットいじめ	→	online (d)
学級崩壊	→	classroom (e)
適応障害	→	(f) disorder
性同一性障害	→	(g) identity disorder
核家族	→	(h) family
育児休暇	→	maternity (i)
共働き世帯	→	(j)-earner household

1. adjustment	2. bullying	3. corporal	4. disintegration
5. dual	6. gender	7. leave	8. nuclear
9. returnee	10. withdrawal		

■問B　(a) ～ (i) にそれぞれ対応する英語表現を下記の語群から選びその番号を記せ。

(a) 不登校	(b) 停学	(c) 過食症
(d) 拒食症	(e) 認知症	(f) 養子縁組
(g) 一神教	(h) 多神教	(i) 無神論

1. adoption	2. anorexia	3. atheism
4. bulimia	5. dementia	6. monotheism
7. polytheism	8. suspension	9. truancy

■問C　空所 (a) ～ (c) にそれぞれ入るべき1語を下記の語群から選びその番号を記せ。

人間国宝	→	living national (a)
世界文化遺産	→	world cultural (b)
文化勲章	→	(c) of Culture

1. heritage	2. Order	3. treasure

From print to the Web ― 紙媒体からウェブの重層的構造へ

新聞協会の調査によると、日本における日刊紙発行部数（一般紙とスポーツ紙の双方を含む。朝刊・夕刊セットは1部と計上）は1999年の約5,376万部から2010年には約4,932万部へと減少傾向にある。今後新聞などの紙媒体が消滅してしまうことはないだろうが、ウェブ・ニュース（オンライン・ニュース）には、新聞にはない魅力がある。すなわち、ウェブ・ニュースは様々なメディアの融合体で、新聞のようにニュースを横並びに読むのではなく、ワン・クリックで様々なメディアや情報に重層的にアクセスすることができる。

このトピックを英文で読んでみよう。

Print journalism will not go extinct. But it will become increasingly difficult to compete against the allure of digital media, where editors can combine text, photos, audio, video, animated graphics, interactive chat, and much more. Online media offer readers more variety. Stories, images, and digital extras can be linked together in layers, with related options just a click away. Instead of arranging stories side by side, the way traditional newspapers do, online news sites link related topics in layers that allow readers to roam from story to story.

通信社　News Agencies (3)

✓　ロシア国営のイタル・タス通信（ITAR-TASS）は、ソビエト連邦時代の1925年に誕生したタス通信（TASS）が母体。冷戦期は、政府の公式情報発信機関だったが、ソビエト崩壊後、規模を縮小。中国の新華社通信 "Xinhua News Agency" も国営で中国政府及び共産党の公式見解を報道。政治問題などについて、報道内容や時間的対応状況から、政府の意向や内部事情などを占うことも多い。

NEWS 8

Disk 2
1

Complaint calls over virus-related scams top 10,000 in Japan

Complaint calls over scams related to the novel coronavirus have topped 10,000 since the start of the domestic outbreak in January, the National Consumer Affairs Center of Japan said Wednesday.

Police, meanwhile, said they have been alerted to a number of crimes exploiting the pandemic, including fraudsters tricking their way into the homes of the growing 5 number of elderly people staying indoors in order to commit theft.

Scams reported to the police also include attempts by imposters to swindle money by pretending over the phone to offer financial relief for damage caused by the COVID-19 disease.

By Tuesday, consumer affairs offices around the country had received 11,030 10 calls on such virus-related incidents since January, when the first domestic infection was confirmed.

Police and local authorities, meanwhile, have raised the alert over an increase of virus-related frauds particularly targeting the elderly.

In late March, a man in his 80s in Tokyo's Katsushika Ward received a call from 15 a woman asking him to prepare his bank card and official seal so he could receive financial aid related to the coronavirus.

Other similar scam phone calls included fake information about insurance covering COVID-19 and bogus claims about the dispatch of an exam kit for the virus or work being under way to remove coronavirus from water pipes. 20

The Tokyo police have asked people not to pick up calls from unknown numbers and to record messages instead, so as to gauge whether the calls are genuine.

There have also been online approaches via emails and text messages pretending to sell expensive face masks or asking the receiver to invest in a fake mask sales business. 25

"Never listen when the story sounds groundless, and please call your local consumer affairs center if you feel any doubt," warned an official of the national center.

— *Based on a report on Kyodo News report on April 9, 2020* —

〈ニュース解説〉 新型コロナウィルスの感染拡大に伴い、人々の不安につけ込んだ詐欺や悪質商法などに関するさまざまな相談が国民生活センター及び全国各地の消費生活センターに寄せられた。不安をあおって現金をだまし取ったり代金を振り込ませたりする詐欺の他、個人情報や口座番号を聞き出す事例なども多く報告されている。

(Notes)

◆ **scam** （信用）詐欺、ぺてん

◆ (L. 2-3) **National Consumer Affairs Center of Japan** 国民生活センター（国民生活の安定と向上のため、生活問題に関する調査・研究、消費者相談、商品テストなどを行う独立行政法人。国に設置され、地方自治体が管理する後述の消費生活センターと国とをつなぐ中核的役割を担っている。後出の "national center" も同義）

◆ (L. 4) **exploit** 〜を悪用する、〜につけ込む

◆ (L. 5) **fraudster** 詐欺師（後出の "fraud" は「詐欺、詐欺行為」の意）

◆ (L. 7) **imposter** （他人になりすます）詐欺師、偽者

◆ (L. 7) **swindle** （金などを）だまして巻き上げる、だまし取る

◆ (L. 8) **financial relief** 助成金、補助金、給付金（後出の "financial aid" も同義）

◆ (L. 10) **consumer affairs office** 消費生活センター（全国の地方自治体が設置する消費者相談窓口。国が管轄する国民生活センターと連携して消費者トラブルの解決支援を行っている。後出の "consumer affairs center" も同義）

◆ (L. 15) **Katsushika Ward** 葛飾区

◆ (L. 19) **bogus** 偽の、いんちきの

◆ (L. 19) **dispatch** （郵便などの）発送

◆ (L. 21) **the Tokyo police** 警視庁 【「警視庁」の正式な英語名称は "the Metropolitan Police Department（略称 MPD）"。"police" は通常、集合的に複数扱い】

◆ (L. 22) **gauge** 判断する

◆ (L. 23) **text message** （携帯電話やスマートフォン同士で送受信する）テキストメッセージ、ショートメッセージ

◆ (L. 26) **groundless** 事実無根の、根拠のない

1. 本文の内容と一致するものには T (True) を、一致しないものには F (False) を記せ。

(   ) (1) At most 10,000 complaint calls related to the spread of COVID-19 have been reported since the disease outbreak started in Japan.

(   ) (2) According to the police and local authorities, women who live alone have been exclusively targeted by scammers.

(   ) (3) The Tokyo police have advised people to record messages from suspicious callers without hanging up.

(   ) (4) Fraudsters prey on people by using various methods such as false impersonation and hoax text messages.

(   ) (5) In order to avoid becoming a victim of a fraud, you should turn to your local consumer affairs center if you receive a dubious message.

2. 下記の犯罪事例の中で本文に<u>記載されていないもの</u>は次のうちどれか。(a)〜(e) から一つ選び記号で答えよ。

(a) unscrupulous sales taking advantage of the unavailability of face masks

(b) telephone swindlers promising money for virus-related damage

(c) gaining entry into homes to steal money or other valuables

(d) imposters pretending to be city officials who ask people to stock up on supplies

(e) calls demanding payment for non-existent goods or services

音声を聞き、下線部を補え。（２回録音されています。１回目はナチュラルスピード、２回目はスロースピードです。）

Natural
3
Slow
5

A Minneapolis policeman, [(1)] _____
_____ George Floyd by kneeling on his neck, was taken into custody Friday and charged with third-degree murder, officials said.

Derek Chauvin is one of four officers who were fired shortly after an explosive video emerged showing a handcuffed Floyd lying on the street as an officer identified as Chauvin [(2)] _____ for at least five minutes on Monday.

The death of the 46-year-old Floyd has sparked [(3)] _____
_____ in Minneapolis and other US cities over police brutality against African-Americans.

Natural
4
Slow
6

So far, hundreds of shops have been damaged and [(4)] _____
_____ .

Overnight, demonstrators broke through law enforcement barriers to overtake the Minneapolis police station where [(5)] _____
_____ were based.

Minnesota's national guard announced that 500 troops were being deployed Friday for peacekeeping amid signs that the anger was nowhere near dissipating.

— *Based on a report on AFP News on May 29, 2020* —

5

10

15

〈ニュース解説〉　米中西部ミネソタ州のミネアポリス市で、警官に膝で首を圧迫され黒人男性が死亡した事件は、激しい抗議運動となって全米に広まった。抗議デモ隊の一部は時に暴徒化し、デモに乗じた商業施設の破壊や略奪、放火なども発生。警察側もデモ隊に催涙ガスを使用するなどし、治安維持のため州兵が派遣される事態となった。米国では警官による黒人への過剰な暴力が長年問題となっており、今回の抗議運動はそういった根深い人種差別への不満が一気に噴出したものと考えられている。繰り返される同様の悲劇に、「黒人の命を軽視するな」との意味合いを込めたスローガン、"Black Lives Matter（黒人の命は大切）" を掲げた抗議運動は世界中に広がっている。

(Notes)

George Floyd ジョージ・フロイド　**take ~ into custody** ~の身柄を拘束する、取り押さえる　**third-degree murder** 第３級殺人罪［第３級殺人罪は「殺害の悪意なしに著しく危険な行為で死に至らしめた」とする罪。その後、第３級殺人罪では軽すぎるとして「計画性のない殺人」を対象とする、より重い「第２級殺人罪」に変更された。なお、「第１級殺人罪」(first-degree murder) は、「計画的な故意による殺人」で、最も罪が重い］　**Derek Chauvin** デレク・ショービン　**police brutality** 警察の蛮行　**national guard** 州兵（軍）（直訳は「国家警備隊」だが、通常は州知事の指揮下にあり、「州兵」と訳される。非常時には大統領令で召集される）　**troops**（通例複数形で）軍部隊　**nowhere near** ~には程遠い、~とはかけ離れている

■問A　空所 (a) ～ (k) にそれぞれ入るべき 1 語を下記の語群から選びその番号を記せ。

業務上過失	→	professional (a)
脱税	→	tax (b)
著作権侵害	→	copyright (c)
フィッシング詐欺	→	(d) scam
おとり捜査	→	(e) operation
捜査令状	→	search (f)
物的証拠	→	(g) evidence
状況証拠	→	(h) evidence
精神鑑定	→	(i) test
冤罪	→	(j) charge
自宅軟禁	→	house (k)

1. arrest	2. circumstantial	3. dodge	4. false
5. infringement	6. negligence	7. phishing	8. physical
9. psychiatric	10. sting	11. warrant	

■問B　(a) ～ (q) にそれぞれ対応する英語表現を下記の語群から選びその番号を記せ。

(a) 重罪	(b) 軽犯罪	(c) 違反	(d) 名誉棄損
(e) 拘留	(f) 窃盗	(g) 万引き	(h) スパイ行為
(i) 贈収賄	(j) 監禁	(k) 襲撃	(l) 自白
(m) 大量殺人	(n) 残虐行為	(o) 銃撃	(p) 刺傷
(q) 脱走者			

1. assault	2. atrocity	3. bribery	4. confession
5. confinement	6. custody	7. defamation	8. espionage
9. felony	10. fugitive	11. massacre	12. misdemeanor
13. offense	14. shooting	15. shoplifting	16. stabbing
17. theft			

■問C　(a) ～ (h) をそれぞれ和訳せよ。

(a) abuse	(b) charge	(c) corruption
(d) fraud	(e) interrogation	(f) ransom
(g) robbery	(h) smuggling	

Broadcast news — 放送ニュースの特質

放送ニュースは、テレビやラジオの映像や音声を通じて視聴者の感情に訴えることができ、現実を生で伝える力がある。視聴者も面倒な記事を読む煩わしさから解放され、頭を使うことが少なくて済むから大人気。新聞や雑誌といった紙媒体のようなニュースの深みや掘り下げはないが、視聴者へのアピール度や即時性（immediacy）といった面では軍配が上がる。なお、最近では従来のテレビやラジオに加えて、インターネットで聴けるネット・ラジオ、携帯音楽プレイヤーに音声データ・ファイルとして配信される "Podcast"（ポッドキャスト）や携帯電話で視聴できる "One-Seg television"（ワンセグ・テレビ）等、放送ニュースのメディアも実に多様化してきている。

このトピックを英文で読んでみよう。

　　TV and radio journalism is neither better nor worse than print journalism. It is just different. Each form of media has strengths and weaknesses. Print journalism provides a level of depth, context and sheer information that television and radio newscasts can not supply. Broadcast journalism, through the power of dramatic video and engaging audio, offers emotional appeal, realism and immediacy that printed stories can not match. Watching or listening to a news broadcast generally requires less intellectual effort than reading a complex news story in a newspaper.

NEWS MEDIA IN THE WORLD

通信社　News Agencies (4)

✓　日本の共同通信社（Kyodo News Service）と時事通信社（JIJI Press）は第2次大戦中の国策通信社・聯合通信が1945年に分割されて出来た、非営利の社団法人。中央、地方の新聞や放送へのニュース記事配信とともに、行政機関や民間会社への情報提供サービスを行っている。近時、アジアを中心に英語による国際的な発信活動にも力を入れている。

NEWS 9

Hefty fines and longer prison terms for reckless driving

Disk 2

7
Armed with stiffer penalties, police put motorists on notice that those who pose a danger to others through reckless driving now face hefty fines and lengthy prison terms.

The June 30th enactment of tougher penalties stems in part from a well-publicized road rage incident three years ago that left a couple dead and their two daughters ₅ injured.

The new measures also address reckless driving that may not have led directly to traffic fatalities or injuries.

The revised Road Traffic Law that went into effect from June 30th defines a new category of driving to interfere with other drivers as an area where tough penalties ₁₀ will be imposed.

Ten types of reckless driving were cited, with two covering driving on expressways. Driving too slowly or suddenly stopping on expressways is now considered a crime if such actions serve as a danger to other vehicles.

Among the eight types of reckless driving on ordinary roads are suddenly hitting ₁₅

the brakes and tailgating another vehicle. Making a sudden lane change, repeatedly honking the car horn, keeping the high beam light directed at the vehicle in front, and other forms of reckless driving are also covered.

When police are summoned to deal with complaints about reckless driving, they will use camcorder video, witness statements, and tire tracks to determine if a ₂₀ driver's behavior interfered with others.

Drivers found guilty of interfering with others face a maximum penalty of three years in prison or a fine of 500,000 yen ($4,600).

The penalties are even stiffer for the two examples of interfering with driving on expressways. Drivers found guilty face a maximum penalty of five years of ₂₅ imprisonment or a fine of 1 million yen.

In either case, the driver's license will be immediately invalidated. Those found guilty of interfering on ordinary roads will have to wait two years to reapply for a license while those caught on expressways face a three-year wait.

— *Based on a report on asahi.com on June 30, 2020* —

〈ニュース解説〉　あおり運転（妨害運転）を新たに罪と定め、厳罰化を盛り込んだ改正道路交通法が 2020 年 6 月 30 日に施行された。改正法以前は、加害者が重大事故につながるような速度で車を運転していたかどうかが要件となっていたが、停車行為や妨害行為が含まれるかどうかについては明確でなかった。近年、相次ぐあおり運転による事故が社会問題化し、摘発の強化・厳罰化を求める声が高まったことが改正法成立につながった。

(Notes)

◆ **hefty**　多額の、高額の

◆ **reckless driving**　無謀な運転、危険運転（本文では「あおり運転（妨害運転)」の意で用いられている）

◆ (L. 1)　**put…on notice**　〜に通告する

◆ (L. 1-2)　**pose a danger to**　〜に危険をもたらす

◆ (L. 4)　**enactment**　（制定された）法律（本文では後述の "revised Road Traffic Law" を指す）

◆ (L. 4)　**stem from**　〜に端を発する、〜が原因である

◆ (L. 5)　**road rage incident three years ago**　3 年前に起きたあおり運転による事故（"road rage" は車の運転中、走行する他の車に対して突然激怒すること。2017 年 6 月 5 日、東名高速道路で一家 4 人が乗ったワゴン車があおられて高速道路上に停車を余儀なくされ、その後、後続の大型トラックに追突された。夫婦は死亡し、子ども二人が負傷した）

◆ (L. 8)　**traffic fatalities**　交通事故による死亡 [「（事故などによる）死亡」を意味する場合、"fatality" は通例複数形で用いられる]

◆ (L. 9)　**revised Road Traffic Law**　改正道路交通法（同法では、あおり運転を「通行を妨害する目的で、交通の危険のおそれがある方法により一定の違反をする行為」と規定している）

◆ (L. 9)　**go into effect**　施行される、実施される

◆ (L. 16)　**tailgate**　〜の後ろにぴったりついて走る

◆ (L. 19)　**summon**　〜を呼び出す

◆ (L. 20)　**camcorder video**　カムコーダー（ドライブレコーダー等）で録画した映像（"camcorder" は "camera" と "recorder" が搭載された携帯用のカメラ一体型ビデオレコーダーのこと。一般的にはドライブレコーダーやビデオカメラを指す）

ニュースを読んで、下記の設問に答えよ。

1. 本文の内容と一致するものには T (True) を、一致しないものには F (False) を記せ。

(　) (1) Acts of road rage have become punishable under the revised Road Traffic Law.

(　) (2) If provocative actions do not lead to a fatal accident, the motorist will not be found guilty.

(　) (3) The recorded image of the accident is likely to be strong evidence.

(　) (4) Violators of the revised Road Traffic Law will be obliged to take a traffic safety course instead of receiving a fine.

(　) (5) Drivers found guilty of reckless driving will not ever be able to renew their licenses.

2. 改正道路交通法に規定された一般道路でのあおり運転に該当しないものは次のうちどれか。本文に記載された内容から判断し、(a) ～ (e) から一つ選んで記号で答えよ。

(a) slamming on the brakes

(b) travelling at low speed

(c) aiming the high beam at the car in front

(d) keep honking unnecessarily

(e) aggressive tailgating

音声を聞き、下線部を補え。（2回録音されています。1回目はナチュラルスピード、2回目はスロースピードです。）

Natural 9 Slow 11

A law banning indoor smoking in principle fully took effect in Japan on Wednesday as the country is racing to ⁽¹⁾_____ going into the Tokyo Olympic and Paralympic Games.

The revised health promotion law bans smoking at restaurants, hotels and offices, ⁽²⁾_____. The law partially went into effect last year, banning smoking at schools, hospitals and government offices.

Cigar bars, private homes and hotel rooms are exempt from the ban.

Natural 10 Slow 12

In addition, customers can smoke ⁽³⁾_____ run by individuals on the condition that they have a capital of 50 million yen or less and a floor space of 100 square meters or less, and they ⁽⁴⁾_____ _____ saying that smoking is allowed.

Penalties include a fine of up to 300,000 yen on people ⁽⁵⁾_____ _____ and a fine of up to 500,000 yen on facility operators who set out ashtrays in nonsmoking establishments.

— *Based on a report on Jiji Press on April 1, 2020* —

〈ニュース解説〉　住宅やホテルの客室などを除くすべての施設や公共交通機関を原則屋内禁煙とする改正健康増進法が 2020 年 4 月 1 日に全面施行された。一部の小規模飲食店には特例措置も設けられているが、これにより多くの人が使用する施設は原則禁煙となり、受動喫煙対策が大幅に強化されることになった。

(Notes)
in principle 原則として　**going into** 〜に向けて　**revised health promotion law** 改正健康増進法
cigar bar シガーバー、喫煙目的のバー

■問A　空所 (a) ～ (i) にそれぞれ入るべき1語を下記の語群から選びその番号を記せ。

陪審制度	→	(a) system
裁判員制度	→	(b) system
裁判長	→	(c) judge
国選弁護人	→	(d) lawyer
執行猶予付き判決	→	(e) sentence
終身刑	→	life (f)
死刑	→	death (g)
刑事訴訟	→	(h) action
民事訴訟	→	(i) action

1. civil	2. court-appointed	3. criminal	4. imprisonment
5. jury	6. lay judge	7. penalty	8. presiding
9. suspended			

■問B　(a) ～ (l) にそれぞれ対応する英語表現を下記の語群から選びその番号を記せ。

(a) 弁護士	(b) 検察官	(c) 原告
(d) 被告	(e) 裁判	(f) 起訴
(g) 証言	(h) 評決	(i) 判決
(j) 有罪判決	(k) 刑罰	(l) 恩赦

1. amnesty	2. conviction	3. defendant	4. judgment
5. lawyer	6. penalty	7. plaintiff	8. prosecution
9. prosecutor	10. testimony	11. trial	12. verdict

■問C　日本の司法制度に関係する (a) ～ (f) の用語をそれぞれ和訳せよ。

(a) Supreme Court

(b) high court

(c) district court

(d) family court

(e) summary court

(f) Supreme Public Prosecutors Office

Radio news reporting — ラジオ・ニュースの難しさ

テレビのような映像がなく、新聞・雑誌のように長々と叙述できないのがラジオのニュース。ラジオの聞き手は何か他のことをしながらラジオ・ニュースを聞いている。そうなると、ニュースも簡潔、そして聞き手の注意を一発で喚起する書き方が要求される。記者には、ニュースを30秒でまとめる技術が求められる。"actuality" または "sound bite"（ニュースで繰り返し放送される録音テープからの抜粋）、"natural sound" または "ambient sound"（周囲の様子を伝えるような音声や環境音）、"lead-in"（ニュース番組の導入部分）等はラジオニュース関連の専門用語。テレビ・ニュースの用語と共通するものも多い。最近はインターネットで聞けるラジオサイトも増え、世界中のラジオ放送を無料で聞くことが出来る。ホームページでは豊富な英文記事の他に、ラジオ・ニュースも聴取できる。BBC World Service（英）、NPR（米）、ABC Radio National（豪）等にアクセスしてオンライン・ラジオ・ニュースを聴いてみよう。

このトピックを英文で読んでみよう。

Radio journalism may be the most challenging form of news reporting. You can not rely on graphics and images as TV reporters do. You can not write long, descriptive sentences and stories as print reporters do. When people are listening to your story on the radio, they are doing it while they dodge traffic, talk on their cellphone, and do their makeup. So radio news writing needs to be as direct and attention-grabbing as possible. Word economy is the key. The best radio reporting is snappy yet eloquent, conversational yet concise, friendly yet authoritative. Most stories at most stations require their reporters to boil everything down to its 30-second essence.

NEWS 10

Disk 2
13

All retailers in Japan required to charge fee for plastic bags from July 1

TOKYO—All retail shops across Japan will be required to charge a fee for plastic shopping bags from July 1 as part of a government initiative to reduce plastic waste that is seriously affecting the oceanic ecosystem.

Nationwide retail outlets, including supermarkets, convenience stores, and department stores, will be required to charge for plastic bags as a general rule. The 5 new policy aims to promote the reduction of plastic waste, which flows into the ocean and has a severe impact on the ecosystem. Japan's Environment Ministry is calling for consumers to use their own reusable bags while setting a goal of raising the proportion of customers who decline receiving plastic bags when purchasing products from the current 30 percent to 60 percent. 10

Charges for disposable plastic bags that have loops or handles for holding them have been made obligatory under the new policy. However, bags that incorporate bioplastic that uses plant-derived matter as its raw material and have little adverse impact on the environment, as well as marine biodegradable plastic that can be easily decomposed, or plastic bags that are durable with a thickness of 0.05 millimeters 15 or more are excluded from charges. For the time being, bags using bioplastic must incorporate at least 25 percent of the material for it to qualify as being exempt from charges. Thin plastic roll bags used for holding fresh food are also exempt from the policy.

14

The prices of shopping bags will be determined by each retailer on their own. 20 Many companies set prices that vary depending on the plastic bags' size, and one bag generally costs less than 10 yen. While major supermarkets like Aeon Retail Co. have already taken the lead to charge for shopping bags, the three convenience store giants of Seven-Eleven Japan Co., FamilyMart Co., and Lawson Inc. will also charge fees for plastic bags from July 1. 25

Under the Act on the Promotion of Sorted Collection and Recycling of Containers and Packaging, which stipulates the plastic bag policy, firms that annually use 50 metric tons or more of packaging and containers made of plastic and other materials are required to report their efforts on reducing plastic waste per fiscal year. Penalty regulations, such as the disclosure of offending company names and fines, 30 have also been included if inappropriate actions are observed, such as continuing to provide plastic bags for free.

— Based on a report on Mainichi.com on June 30, 2019 —

〈ニュース解説〉　世界では年間 800 万トンのプラスチックごみが海に流れ込んでいると言われる。中でも海中で砕けて 5 ミリ以下の大きさになったマイクロプラスチックは魚や海鳥の体内からも検出されており、食物連鎖を通じて人間の体内にも蓄積される懸念がある。日本政府はこうした事態に対応するため、プラスチック資源循環戦略を打ち出し、2030 年までに使い捨てプラスチックの排出を累積で 25％抑制する、2035 年までに使用済みプラスチックを 100％再利用、リサイクル等で有効利用する、2030 年までにバイオマスプラスチックを 200 万トン導入するなどの目標を掲げている。今回のレジ袋有料化義務化もその一環で、消費者にライフスタイルの変革を促している。

(Notes)

◆ (L. 1-2)　**plastic shopping bag**　レジ袋（単に "plastic bag" と言われる場合もある）

◆ (L. 7)　**Japan's Environment Ministry**　環境省（正式名称は "Ministry of the Environment"）

◆ (L. 8)　**reusable bag**　再利用可能な袋（日本語では「マイバッグ」、「エコバッグ」とも呼ばれている）

◆ (L. 11)　**disposable plastic bag**　使い捨てのレジ袋

◆ (L. 11)　**loops or handles for holding them**　（レジ袋の「持ち手」を意味する）

◆ (L. 13)　**bioplastic that uses plant-derived matter as its raw material**　（従来のように石油由来ではなく、トウモロコシやサトウキビなどの植物を原材料としたバイオマスプラスチック）

◆ (L. 14)　**marine biodegradable plastic**　海洋生分解性プラスチック（海中の微生物などで自然に水と二酸化炭素に分解されていく環境にやさしいプラスチック）

◆ (L. 18)　**thin plastic roll bags used for holding fresh food**　生鮮食料品など入れるのに使われるロール状の薄いポリ袋

◆ (L. 26)　**Act on Promotion of Sorted Collection and Recycling of Containers and Packaging**　「容器包装に係る分別収集及び再商品化の促進等に関する法律」

　　ニュースを読んで、下記の設問に答えよ。

1. 本文の内容と一致するものには T (True) を、一致しないものには F (False) を記せ。

（　　）(1) The Japanese government introduced a new policy to protect the ocean ecosystem by reducing plastic waste.

（　　）(2) Plastic bags containing at least 50 percent of biomass or ocean biodegradable materials are excluded from the new policy introduced on July 1, 2020.

（　　）(3) Retailers should charge for plastic shopping bags regardless of their thickness.

（　　）(4) The government will decide the prices of plastic shopping bags depending on their size.

（　　）(5) Companies that use a huge amount of plastic packaging and plastic containers might be fined if they do not comply with the law stipulating waste collection and container recycling requirements.

2. 中国は 2017 年末に環境面への配慮からプラスチックごみの輸入を禁止した。その後東南アジア諸国もそれに追従してプラスチックごみの輸入規制を導入する中、日本企業はプラスチックのリサイクル施設への投資を増やしている。下記はそうした事情を報じる Nikkei Asia（2019 年 1 月 12 日付）の一部。語群から適語を空所に補充して英文を完成させること。

Japanese [(1)]_____ are pouring investment into plastic recycling [(2)]_____ to handle the rise in [(3)]_____ and used home electronics remaining in the country following China's near-total ban on imports of plastic waste. Japan [(4)]_____ 9.03 million tons of plastic waste in 2017. About one-tenth of the volume—900,000 tons—was [(5)]_____ to China, which received 70 percent of Japan's plastic waste [(6)]_____.　China banned plastic waste [(7)]_____ at the end of 2017 to reduce pollution from the recycling process. Shipments from Japan to China [(8)]_____ to a mere 2,000 tons monthly in 2018 from a peak of 86,000 tons in August 2017. Finding alternative [(9)]_____ is difficult as other Asian countries tighten regulations on plastic waste.

bottles,　　companies,　　destinations,　　exports,　　facilities,
fell,　　generated,　　imports,　　shipped

音声を聞き、下線部を補え。（２回録音されています。１回目はナチュラルスピード、２回目はスロースピードです。）

Natural
15
Slow
17

Natural
16
Slow
18

TOKYO—As mines around the world slow output in response to the coronavirus pandemic, threatening tighter supplies of precious metals, one resource-poor country is ready to step into the void: Japan.

Mountains of discarded electronics here contain tons of not only gold and silver, but also such industrial metals as the ⁽¹⁾ _____. In terms of gold alone, these hidden reserves are estimated at around 6,800 tons, more than the underground deposits in South Africa.

While Japan's urban mining gained prominence with a pledge to make Olympic medals using recycled metals from discarded electronics, the effort has been building up for years. Processing of discarded electronics ⁽²⁾ _____ to fiscal 2018, reaching about 370,000 tons, according to the Japan Mining Industry Association.

As the metal industry gets serious about urban mining, there is also ⁽³⁾ _____. Metal recycling has already drawn much attention internationally, and competition for discarded circuit boards is projected to heat up.

In comparison with precious metals, whose contents are high in circuit boards, the ⁽⁴⁾ _____. The bottlenecks are contained in the expenses of sorting, dismantling and retrieval. There is currently no low-cost method of sorting and analyzing discarded circuit boards for salvageable content. The process ⁽⁵⁾ _____. The search for labor-saving solutions has become a matter of urgency.

— *Based on a report on asia.nikkei.com on June 9, 2020* —

5

10

15

20

〈ニュース解説〉　東京オリンピック・パラリンピックで授与されるメダルをすべて廃家電や携帯電話から作るというプロジェクトで注目を集めたアーバン・マイニング（都市鉱山）だが、非資源国・日本にとっての有望分野として成長しつつある。

(Notes)
precious metals 貴金属（金属は鉄、銅、鉛、アルミニウムのように大量生産・大量使用されるベース・メタル、希少で耐腐食性がある金、銀、プラチナ等の貴金属、地球上の存在量が稀少か抽出困難であるが産業に利用されることが多いリチウムやチタン等のレア・メタルに大別される）　**a pledge to make Olympic medals out of recycled electronics**（2017年4月から2019年3月まで行われた「都市鉱山からつくる！みんなのメダルプロジェクト」を指す。このプロジェクトでは2020年7－8月に予定されていた東京オリンピック・パラリンピックで使用される約5000個のメダルに必要な金・銀・銅を使用ずみの携帯電話等の小型家電機器から抽出すべく回収することを目指し、必要な金属量に見合う機器の回収に成功した）　**Japan Mining Industry Association** 日本鉱業協会　**discarded circuit board** 廃基板

■問A 空所 (a) 〜 (g) にそれぞれ入るべき1語を下記の語群から選びその番号を記せ。

光化学スモッグ	→	(a) smog
酸性雨	→	(b) rain
生物多様性	→	biological (c)
排ガス規制	→	(d) control
産業廃棄物	→	(e) waste
放射線廃棄物	→	(f) waste
液化天然ガス	→	(g) natural gas

1. acid　　　　　2. diversity　　　　3. emission
4. industrial　　5. liquefied　　　　6. photochemical
7. radioactive

■問B (a) 〜 (l) をそれぞれ和訳せよ。

(a) solar cell

(b) renewable energy

(c) geothermal power production

(d) wave-energy power station

(e) hydroelectric generation

(f) thermal power plant

(g) Nuclear Regulation Authority

(h) ecosystem

(i) ozone layer depletion

(j) environmentalist

(k) environmentally friendly

(l) pollutant

Media convergence ― メディアの融合化への流れ

昨今のジャーナリズムは、マルチメディアを駆使して情報を伝達する。1つのことを伝えるにも、写真、オーディオ、ビデオ（動画）、テキスト（文字データ）というようにあらゆる媒体を使って、より理想に近い情報を作り出し伝達することが出来るのがメディア融合の強みである。

このトピックを英文で読んでみよう。

Suppose you decided to profile Ludwig van Gogh, a brilliant painter and composer. Which medium, or media, would produce the best story? To display his paintings, you would use photographs. To present his music, you would use audio recordings. To show him at work—conducting an orchestra or painting—you would use video footage. To explain the meaning and impact of his art, you would use text. In short, to create the ideal profile, you would need multimedia. Cross-platform journalism, media convergence—whatever you call it, it is an idea whose time has finally come.

NEWS MEDIA IN THE WORLD

新聞社 Newspapers (1)

✔ 英国では、庶民を読者とする大衆紙には昔からタブロイド判（tabloid）が多いが、これまで大判（broadsheet）で出されていた高級紙 *Times* や *Guardian* も判型をタブロイド判に変えつつある。2015 年以降日本経済新聞傘下にある高級経済紙 *Financial Times*（略称 FT）は大判でピンク色の用紙が特徴。近年経費削減等の理由から紙面の縮小が流行で、*Guardian* やフランスの *Le Monde* など、大判とタブロイド判の中間の大きさのベルリーナ判（Berliner format）を採用する新聞もあった。*Guardian* は、その後 2018 年に判型をベルリーナ判からタブロイド判に変更し、*Times* と並び英国高級紙のタブロイド判化として話題となった。

Chapter 11　気象・災害

NEWS 11

Disk 2

19 **Permafrost collapse is speeding climate change, study warns**

PARIS—Permafrost in Canada, Alaska, and Siberia is abruptly crumbling in ways that could release large stores of greenhouse gases more quickly than anticipated, researchers have warned.

Scientists have long fretted that climate change, which has heated Arctic and subarctic regions at double the global rate, will release planet-warming carbon 5 dioxide and methane that have remained safely locked inside frozen landscapes for millenniums. It was assumed this process would be gradual, leaving humanity time to reduce carbon emissions enough to prevent a vicious circle of melting ice and global warming. But a study published in Nature Geoscience says projections of how much carbon would be released by this kind of slow and steady thawing overlook a 10 less well-known process whereby certain types of icy terrain disintegrate suddenly, sometimes within days.

"Although abrupt permafrost thawing will occur in less than 20 percent of frozen land, it increases permafrost carbon release projections by about 50 percent," said lead author Merritt Turetsky, head of the Institute of Arctic and Alpine Research in 15 Colorado.

Permafrost contains rocks, soil, sand, and pockets of pure ground ice. Its rich **20** carbon content is the remains of life that once flourished in the arctic, including plants, animals and microbes. This matter—which never fully decomposed—has been frozen for thousands of years. 20

It stretches across an area nearly as big as Canada and the US combined and holds 1.5 trillion tons of carbon, twice as much as in the atmosphere and three times the amount humanity has emitted since the start of industrialization. Some of this once rock-solid ground has begun to soften, upending indigenous communities and threatening industrial infrastructure across the subarctic region, especially in Russia. 25

The evidence is mixed as to whether this permafrost has started to vent significant quantities of methane or carbon dioxide. Projections are also uncertain, with some scientists saying future emissions may be at least partially offset by new vegetation, which absorbs and stores carbon dioxide. But there is no doubt, experts say, that permafrost will continue to give way as temperatures climb. 30

— Based on a report on AFP-Jiji on Japantimes.com on February 6, 2020 —

〈ニュース解説〉　地球温暖化による気温上昇で北方の永久凍土が融解し、そこに内包されている温室効果ガスが放出され、さらなる地球温暖化を徐々に招く可能性があることはかねてから指摘されていた。しかし、コロラド大学の研究者等が永久凍土には急速に融解する部分があり、従来考えられていたよりも大きな影響を急激に地球温暖化にもたらす可能性があると警告する調査結果を発表した。これによりパリ協定に定められた温室効果ガスの排出削減目標達成はますます難しくなることが懸念される。また、永久凍土には様々な古代生物の死骸や病原菌、ウイルスなども凍結されていると言われ、融解によりこれらが溶け出すことも懸念される。

(Notes)

◆　**Permafrost**　永久凍土（"permanent" と "frost" からできた語。北極圏やシベリアなどに見られ、決して溶けないとされていたが、温暖化による溶解例が最近見られようになった）

◆　(L. 4)　**fret**　心配する（"worry" と同義）

◆　(L. 5)　**subarctic regions**　北極に近い亜北極地域

◆　(L. 7)　**millennium**　1000 年間（"millenniums" は非常に長い期間、数千年、何千年を意味する）

◆　(L. 8)　**vicious cycle**　悪循環

◆　(L. 9)　**Nature Geoscience**　ネイチャー・ジオサイエンス誌（Nature Publishing Group が月 1 回発行する地球科学全般をカバーする学術誌）

◆　(L. 11)　**terrain**　土地、地層（"land", "ground" と同義。ラテンン語で大地、地球を表す "terra" から）

◆　(L. 15)　**lead author**　主執筆者、代表執筆者

◆　(L. 15-16)　**Merritt Turetsuky, head of the Institute of Arctic and Alpine Research in Colorado**—　米コロラド大学北極高山研究所のメリット・ツレツキー所長（同研究所は同大学ボルダー校に 1951 年設立。略称：INSTAAR）

◆　(L. 17)　**pockets**　（周辺の他所とは異なる性質を持つ部分などを指す）

◆　(L. 18)　**remains**　死骸、残骸（"remains" は不可算名詞として使われる）

◆　(L. 19)　**microbe**　微生物

◆　(L. 23)　**since the start of industrialization**　産業革命開始以来

◆　(L. 28-29)　**new vegetation**　新たに生える植物

ニュースを読んで、下記の設問に答えよ。

1. 本文の内容と一致するものには T (True) を、一致しないものには F (False) を記せ。

(   ) (1) Temperatures in the arctic and subarctic regions have been rising much faster than in the rest of the world.

(   ) (2) Permafrost can be found only in the US and Canada.

(   ) (3) Some scientists are concerned about the possibility that permafrost will thaw abruptly, releasing a lot of carbon dioxide and methane.

(   ) (4) Abrupt thawing will likely happen in the permafrost zone all over the world.

(   ) (5) It is certain that permafrost will continue to melt because of global warming.

2. 下記は National Geographic 誌に掲載された "permafrost" についての説明の一部だが、下記の語群から空所に適語を補充して英文を完成させること。

Permafrost is a permanently (1.   ) layer below the Earth (2.   ). It consists of soil, gravel, and sand, usually bound together by (3.   ). Permafrost usually remains at or below 0℃ for at least two (4.   ). Its (5.   ) can range from 1 meter to more than 1,000 meters. Permafrost covers approximately 22.8 million (6.   ) kilometers in the Earth's Northern Hemisphere.

frozen,   ice,   square,   surface,   thickness,   years

音声を聞き、下線部を補え。（２回録音されています。１回目はナチュラルスピード、２回目はスロースピードです。）

Natural 21 Slow 23

A swarm of desert locusts clouded the skies in the Indian city of Gurgaon on Saturday, prompting the government of the Indian capital New Delhi to issue an advisory informing officials to remain on high alert.

The insects swept through the city at 11:30 a.m. local time, a resident who lives in Gurgaon told CNN. After 15 minutes, thousands of locusts [(1)]

_____ before being swept away by high winds.

In neighboring New Delhi, the city's Labor and Development Minister, Gopal Rai, shared an advisory on Twitter, stating that all district magistrates in New Delhi are advised "to remain on high alert" as [(2)]

_____ the migratory pest. On June 20, the Food and Agriculture Organization (FAO) of the United Nations said that India should remain on high alert during the next four weeks.

Natural 22 Slow 24

The desert locust is among the most destructive of migratory pests because of its speed and ability to multiply rapidly. Adult locusts can fly up to 150 kilometers (93 miles) a day and eat their own body weight—equal to 2 grams— [(3)]

_____ .

East Africa is seeing the worst locust outbreak in decades, after [(4)]

_____ of the biblical pest. Spraying pesticide is the most effective way of killing locusts, but the coronavirus pandemic has slowed efforts to tackle the outbreak on the African continent.

— *Based on a report on CNN.com on June 27, 2020* —

〈ニュース解説〉 2019年以来東アフリカを中心に大量発生しつづけてる害虫サバクトビバッタは2020年6月現在、インド洋を越えてパキスタン、インドにまで到達している。インド・パキスタンは大型のサイクロンによる大雨に襲われた影響からサバクトビバッタが繁殖しやすい環境になっている。サバクトビバッタは穀物や野菜等を食い荒らす害虫で、ケニア、ソマリア、エチオピア等東アフリカでも食の安全保障が脅かされる事態になっている。インドやパキスタンでもバッタの猛威が食料不足につながることがコロナ禍に加えて懸念されている。

(Notes)

desert locust サバクトビバッタ（学名は "Schistocerca gregaria"。生まれた砂漠地帯に異常気象による降雨あると植物が異常繁殖し、このバッタも異常繁殖する。さらに一定に密度を超えると「突然群生相」に変異し移動能力を持つ） **Indian city of Gurgaon** インドの都市グルガオン（北インドのビジネス都市） **the government of the Indian capital New Delhi** 首都圏政府（首都ニューデリーならびに周辺地域を管轄する政府で、首都の南西に位置するグルガオンもその管轄地域の一つ） **the city's Labor and Development Minister Gopal Rai** 首都圏政府のゴパル・ライ労働開発大臣 **district magistrates** ここでは首都圏政府管轄下にある地域・地区のトップを指す **Food and Agriculture Organization**（国連）食糧農業機関（世界各国国民の栄養水準及び生活水準の向上、食料及び農産物の生産及び流通の改善、農村住民の生活条件の改善を通じて世界経済の発展と人類の飢餓からの解放を目的とし1945年に設立された国連の専門機関。本部はローマ。2019年8月現在、194か国ならびにEUが加盟） **biblical pest** [（旧約）聖書にもバッタの大群の襲来が記されていることを意味する]

■問A (a) 〜 (d) のカタカナ語を英語で記せ。

(a) トリアージ

(b) ヘクトパスカル

(c) マグニチュード

(d) ハリケーン

■問B (a) 〜 (r) にそれぞれ対応する英語表現を下記の語群から選びその番号を記せ。

(a) （日本の）気象庁　　　　　(b) 天気予報

(c) 天気図　　　　　　　　　　(d) 気象衛星

(e) 洪水警報　　　　　　　　　(f) 津波警報

(g) 雪崩　　　　　　　　　　　(h) 干ばつ

(i) 寒波　　　　　　　　　　　(j) 熱波

(k) 余震　　　　　　　　　　　(l) 火山噴火

(m) 溶岩流　　　　　　　　　　(n) 地滑り

(o) 低気圧　　　　　　　　　　(p) 避難所

(q) 救助隊　　　　　　　　　　(r) 救急車

1. aftershock　　　　　　　　2. ambulance
3. avalanche　　　　　　　　4. cold wave
5. drought　　　　　　　　　6. flood warning
7. heat wave　　　　　　　　8. Japan Meteorological Agency
9. landslide　　　　　　　　10. lava flow
11. low pressure (system)　　12. rescuers
13. shelter　　　　　　　　　14. tidal wave warning
15. volcanic eruption　　　　16. weather chart
17. weather forecast　　　　18. weather satellite

　Chapter 1-10 ではニュースの定義から始めて、ニュースの種類、ニュースの構成要素と組み立て方といったポイントを概観すると共に、紙媒体のニュース、オンラインニュース、映像や音声で伝えるニュースの特質と、これらのニュースの融合化の流れを紹介した。Chapter 11-15 ではジャーナリストがひとつひとつの表現や文章を書く上で留意すべき 5 つの重要点を検討する。

Passive verbs ― 受身の動詞

即時性や解り易さを旨とする英文ジャーナリズムの世界では、より直接的で、迫力のある文章を作るため、能動態を用い、動詞の受身用法（be ＋過去分詞）は避けるべき、というのが常識。
　受身用法は、
- ➢　主張内容があいまいになり、文章にインパクトがなくなる
- ➢　主語や主体がわかりにくく、誰の意見か不明で無責任な内容になりやすい
- ➢　There is 〜や There are 〜を使う表現は読者に迂遠で慇懃な感じを与える
- ➢　能動態より be 動詞と動作主を示す by が増えることで文章が長くなる

などのデメリットがある。
パンチのあるニュース記事を書くためには、力強く、直接的でイメージのわく動詞を選ぶ事も大切だ。

このトピックを英文で読んでみよう。

　There is a problem many reporters struggle with. The sentences that are written by them are passive. Their phrasing is made awkward because of this, and—wait! *Stop!*

　Let's rewrite that paragraph to make it less *passive*:

　Many reporters struggle because they write passive sentences. This makes their phrasing awkward.

　See the difference? We have strengthened our syntax by starting sentences with their subjects. We have eliminated that clunky phrase *there is*. And we have replaced the verb *to be* (words such as *is* and *are*), with stronger verbs.

　You do not have to be a grammar geek to see our point here. Make your sentences *emphatic*. Avoid weak, flabby verbs.

NEWS MEDIA IN THE WORLD

新聞社　Newspapers (2)

✓　米国の新聞は発行部数の少ない地域紙が主流。リベラルな高級紙といわれる *New York Times* や *Washington Post*、*Los Angeles Times* も地方紙だ。米国では、地方紙で研鑽を積んだ記者が高級紙や全国放送の記者に採用されるのが一般的。1980 年代に全米を対象に創刊された *USA Today* も各地域のニュースをフォロー。経済紙の *Wall Street Journal*（略称 WSJ）は、経済通信社の Dow Jones の所有。保守的論調で知られる。

NEWS 12

Disk 2

25 **Steepening birthrate decline defies policy support**

TOKYO—Japan on Friday announced its lowest fertility rate since 2007, marking four years of decline and underscoring a persistent challenge that countries from South Korea to France have yet to solve.

Japan's total fertility rate, the average number of children a woman will give birth to in her lifetime, dropped 0.6 point to 1.36 last year, though it remains above 5 the record low of 1.26 set in 2005. Tokyo logged the lowest rate of any of the country's regions, reaching just 1.15.

The country's decades-long downtrend in fertility rates is a problem shared by advanced economies across Asia and the world. It shows little sign of stopping and could fall further as the pandemic wreaks havoc on the global economy. 10

"The difficulties that younger generations face in establishing families have not improved," said population expert Ryuichi Kaneko, a professor at Meiji University in Tokyo. "There will probably be couples who put off having children because of the coronavirus. It's possible that the number and rate of births could go even lower going forward." 15

South Korea's total fertility rate fell below 1 for the first time in 2018 and reached a worldwide low of 0.92 last year, suggesting that government efforts to **26** encourage child-rearing have done little good.

France saw its fertility rate fall to 1.88 in 2018 from 2.01 in 2008, below the level of about 2 needed to sustain a population. This is despite generous benefits for 20 new parents that had been seen as a potential solution to the demographic challenge.

A decline in childbearing among those in their 20s indicates that "women are focusing on their careers and delaying childbirth," said Megumu Murakami of the Japan Research Institute.

Promoting work styles that are compatible with raising children remains a 25 challenge in Japan as well. For parental leave to become more widespread, new parents need the freedom to step away from work or cut back their hours before returning to full-time positions.

— Based on a report on asia.nikkei.com on June 6, 2019 —

〈ニュース解説〉　2019年の人口動態統計によると、合計特殊出生率（15歳から49歳の女性1人が生涯に産む子供の数）は4年連続低下し、1.36人となった。政府は教育の無償化や保育園の充実など、少子化対策に年間約5兆円を投じているが、奏功していない。

(Notes)

◆ (L. 1) **fertility rate** 合計特殊出生率［正式には total fertility rate（合計特殊出生率）。「出生率」はこれとは異なり、その年に生まれた人口1000人当たりの出生数］

◆ (L. 8) **The country's decades-long downtrend in fertility rates** （日本では1975年頃から少子化現象が続いている。合計特殊出生率は戦後ベビーブーム時の1947年には4.54人を記録したが、その後低下。1975年には2.0人を下回った。過去最低値は2005年の1.26人。その後団塊ジュニア世代が出産適齢期を迎え一旦上向いたが、2016年以降また低下が続いている）

◆ (L. 10) **wreak havoc on ～** ～に大混乱をもたらす、大きな被害が生じる

◆ (L. 12) **Ryuichi Kaneko, a professor at Meiji University** 金子隆一明治大学教授

◆ (L. 16) **South Korea's total fertility rate fell below 1 for the first time in 2018** （韓国では2015年から出生率の低下が続いている。未婚人口比率が上昇し、結婚しても子供を持たない夫婦も増えてきている）

◆ (L. 19) **France saw its fertility rate fall to 1.88 in 2018 from 2.01 in 2008** （フランスは少子化対策が功を奏した先進国として知られているが、近年出生率が低下してきている。その理由としては、政府の経済支援策の後退や女性の高学歴化などがあげられている）

◆ (L. 23-24) **Megumi Murakami of the Japan Research Institute** 日本総研（株式会社日本総合研究所）の村上芽研究員

◆ (L. 26) **parental leave** 男女いずれもが取得できる育児休暇、育休（女性の産休は maternity leave）

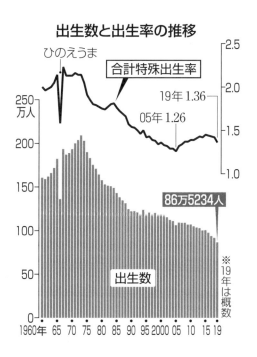

出生数と出生率の推移

1. 本文の内容と一致するものには T (True) を、一致しないものには F (False) を記せ。

(   ) (1) The South Korean government has not taken measures to stop a decline in its birth rate.

(   ) (2) Japan recorded the lowest total fertility rate in 2019.

(   ) (3) An expert predicted that both the number of births and birth rates will be affected by the coronavirus outbreak.

(   ) (4) France's birth rate has been steadily increasing because of generous support provided by the government.

(   ) (5) In Japan, new parents still have difficult taking parental leave.

2. 本文ではコロナ禍が日本の出生率に及ぼす影響が言及されているが、ブルッキングス研究所は、出生行動を経済面から分析した調査から分かったことや 2007 年～2009 年の世界的金融不況時、スペイン風邪流行時のデータなどをベースに、新型コロナウイルスが米国の出生数を 30 万～50 万人の規模で落ち込ませる可能性があるとの推計を発表した。以下はそれを報じた CNN.com の記事の一部。下記の語群から空所に適語を補充して英文を完成させること。

The ($^{1.}$) in births could be on the ($^{2.}$) of 300,000 to 500,000 fewer ($^{3.}$) next year. We base this expectation on ($^{4.}$) drawn from economic studies of ($^{5.}$) behavior, along with ($^{6.}$) presented here from the Great Recession of 2007-2009 and the 1918 Spanish flu.

> births,   data,   decline,   fertility,   lessons,   order

音声を聞き、下線部を補え。（２回録音されています。１回目はナチュラルスピード、２回目はスロースピードです。）

27
Slow
29

A recent survey has found that 70 percent of respondents are in favor of telecommuting [1] _____, with many happy with the reduction in commuting. Those in favor comprise 24.8 percent who fully think telecommuting should be promoted and 45.2 percent who somewhat think so. 5

Asked to describe good things about remote work, [2] _____ _____, 68.2 percent said there is no stress from commuting and 50.6 percent said they can live in and work from places with cheaper housing costs.

Being able to work even when caring for family members or others was mentioned by 47.7 percent, [3] _____ 10 _____ by 42.4 percent, and better working environments for people with physical disabilities by 41.6 percent.

28
Slow
30

Asked to describe problems with remote work, 71.9 percent said there is work that has to be done at the office, and 39.1 percent said the lack of workplace interaction may [4] _____. 15

Other problems included difficulties communicating with bosses and coworkers (35.8 percent), [5] _____ _____ during work (30.0 percent), and higher utility and food costs (29.9 percent).

— Based on a report on Jiji on Japantimes.com on June 22, 2020 —

〈ニュース解説〉 コロナ禍で一気に進んだテレワーク。コロナ後もテレワークを新常態とすることを目指す企業もある。政府も経済界と連携し、テレワークや移住を支援し地方創成、東京一極集中の是正を図ろうとしている。

(Notes)

a recent survey（2020 年 5 月に時事通信が実施した「労働に関する世論調査」。全国 18 歳以上の 2000人を対象に行われ、有効回収率は 51.3 パーセントだった） **telecommuting**［テレワーク（telework）、リモートワーク（remote work）と同義］ **respondents** 回答者 **cheaper housing costs** 安い住宅コスト（都心から離れた郊外に居住することで家賃が安く済むことなど） **physical disabilities** 身体的障害

■問A　空所 (a) ～ (g) にそれぞれ入るべき1語を下記の語群から選びその番号を記せ。

合計特殊出生率	→	total (a) rate
幼児死亡率	→	infant (b)
人口密度が高い地域	→	(c) populated area
人口密度が低い地域	→	(d) populated area
人口過密地域	→	(e) area
過疎化地域	→	(f) area
人口動向	→	(g) trend

1. demographic　　2. densely　　3. depopulated　　4. fertility
5. mortality　　6. overpopulated　　7. sparsely

■問B　(a) ～ (l) をそれぞれ和訳せよ。

(a) equal employment opportunity

(b) emerging countries

(c) least developed countries

(d) income gap

(e) social security

(f) average life expectancy

(g) minimum wage

(h) ratio of job offers to seekers

(i) pension

(j) health insurance

(k) nursing home

(l) gerontology

Redundancy ── 冗長な文章を避ける

不必要な語や表現を使用すると文章は冗長になる。例えば、形容詞と名詞の組み合わせでは、名詞にその形容詞の意味がもとから含まれている場合にその表現は冗長となる。副詞と動詞の組み合わせにおいても、動詞がその副詞の意味を持つ場合に同様の問題が発生する。ニュースルームでは、記者が作成したニュース原稿は編集デスクに送られ文体や内容のチェックを受けた後、報道される。

このトピックを英文で読んでみよう。

Sometimes it is not so obvious that you are using unnecessary words and phrases. Why say that someone is *currently* president of the club? Or that the game is *scheduled for* Friday night? Or that the victims were burned *in the flames*?

Those italicized words add bulk, but no extra meaning. Just as bad are phrases such as these, which are simply doublespeak:

grateful thanks	true fact	personal opinion
all-time record	end result	serious danger
totally destroyed	very unique	first time ever

Be on the lookout for unnecessary modifiers that *sound* logical but add nothing. Eliminate waste. Edit yourself ruthlessly. As Mark Twain once advised: "When in doubt, strike it out."

新聞社 Newspapers (3)

✔ ロシアのプラウダ（*Pravda*）、中国の人民日報（*People's Daily*）はいずれも両国共産党の機関紙として出発。ソビエト崩壊や中国の近代化により情報発信の多様化が進んだが、報道活動に一定の制限がある中国では政府の意向を窺うメディアとして依然重要。アジアでは、シンガポールの英字紙 *Straits Times* や華字紙の『聯合早報』、タイの英字紙 *Nation*、日本の英字紙 *Japan Times* 等がある。FT や WSJ のアジア版、*New York Times* の世界版である *International New York Times*（かつての *International Herald Tribune*）等が各地で印刷発行されている。

NEWS 13

Disk 2
(31)

Asteroid as powerful as 10 billion WWII atomic bombs may have wiped out the dinosaurs

Scientists have discovered evidence that the impact of an asteroid as powerful as 10 billion World War II-era atomic bombs caused the extinction of the dinosaurs. The 7.5-mile (12-km) wide asteroid struck the Earth 66 million years ago and caused 75% of life on the planet to become extinct, according to research led by the University of Texas and published in the PNAS journal.   5

It is thought the event triggered wildfires over 900 miles away, as well as sparking a devastating tsunami. Many dinosaurs would have died that day, but others may have perished from the atmospheric fall-out that followed. Scientists think the earth cooled dramatically after sulfur was released into the atmosphere, blocking the sun and killing off life.   10

The new research was based on rocks collected in 2016 from the Chicxulub impact site off the coast of the Yucatan Peninsula in Mexico. Professor Sean Gulick, who led the study, told CNN: "For me, personally, successfully collecting the cores from the peak ring of the Chicxulub crater was the fruit of years of proposal writing
(32)
and planning made reality. It was a truly exciting moment when we first encountered 15 the sediments from the impact itself and, moreover, when we realized we were seeing events in such detail."

Gulick added that the project presented an unusual opportunity for geologists to read the "rock record," as 130 meters of rock in the crater represented the events of the single day when the asteroid struck. Typically, one centimeter of rock represents 20 every 1,000 years.

Gulick and his team concluded, from the abundance of sulfur-rich rocks near the crater and their absence within it, that the asteroid must have vaporized any sulfur previously present. They estimate that 325 billion metric tons or more of sulfur were ejected into the atmosphere after the giant rock's impact. This is four orders of 25 magnitude greater than the amount released by Krakatoa's eruption in 1883, which caused a 2.2 degrees Fahrenheit average temperature drop for five years.

— Based on a report on CNN.com on September 10, 2019 —

〈ニュース解説〉 今から 6600 万年前、メキシコのユカタン半島沖に巨大な小惑星が衝突、その影響で恐竜が地球上から姿を消したという説が有力であった。しかし、それがどのような過程を経て起きたのかは、長い間謎に包まれてきた。近年、科学者たちはこの謎を解くべく、衝突後のクレーターの詳細な地質調査を実施して、小惑星衝突が引き起こした負の連鎖反応を明らかにした。

(Notes)

◆ **asteroid** 小惑星

◆ **WWII** 第 2 次世界大戦（World War II）

◆ (L. 4-5) **University of Texas** テキサス大学オースティン校（正式名：The University of Texas at Austin テキサス州オースティンに本部を置く米国の州立大学）

◆ (L. 5) **PNAS journal** 米国科学アカデミー紀要（正式名：Proceedings of the National Academy of Sciences of the United States of America。自然科学、社会科学、人文科学分野のインパクトが大きい論文を数多く掲載する）

◆ (L. 8) **atmospheric fall-out** 大気中の粉塵や煤など

◆ (L. 9) **sulfur** 硫黄

◆ (L. 11-12) **Chicxulub impact site** チシュルーブ・クレーター（チシュルーブの小惑星落下地点）

◆ (L. 12) **Yucatan Peninsula** ユカタン半島（メキシコ湾とカリブ海との間に突き出ている半島でメキシコ、グアテマラ、ベリーズにまたがる）

◆ (L. 12) **Sean Gulick** ショーン・グリック

◆ (L. 13) **core** 地質資料、地質サンプル（地層の構成を調査するために、パイプの形状をしたドリルを地層に挿入して採取した円柱状の土壌サンプル）

◆ (L. 14) **peak ring** ピーク・リング（クレーターの中央部の環状に盛り上がった部分）

◆ (L. 16) **sediments** 堆積物

◆ (L. 18) **geologist** 地質学者

◆ (L. 19) **"rock record"** 「岩石に残された記録」

◆ (L. 19) **130 meters of rock** 130 メートルの岩石の層

◆ (L. 23) **vaporize** 気化する

◆ (L. 25-26) **four orders of magnitude** 1 万倍（order of magnitude は「桁」の意味。one order of magnitude は増加の場合は 10 倍、減少の場合には 10 分の 1 になることを意味する）

◆ (L. 26) **Krakatoa** クラカタウ（インドネシアのジャワ島とスマトラ島の中間、スンダ海峡にある火山島の総称で、ランプン州に属する）

◆ (L. 27) **Fahrenheit** 華氏

ニュースを読んで、下記の設問に答えよ。

1. 本文の内容と一致するものには T (True) を、一致しないものには F (False) を記せ。

(   ) (1) A group of scientists believe that the collision of an asteroid with the Earth resulted both directly and indirectly in the total disappearance of the dinosaurs.

(   ) (2) The research published in the PNAS journal claims that disastrous events, independent of one another, led up to the extinction of dinosaurs.

(   ) (3) It appears that dinosaurs became extinct due to the collision of an asteroid that produced both high and then low temperatures.

(   ) (4) The conclusion that the researchers arrived at was derived from the samples of rock collected from under the sea.

(   ) (5) Prof. Gulick said that some rocks lying on the floor of the crater offered a clue to how dinosaurs had been killed.

2. 次の英文を完成させるために、(a) 〜 (d) から最も適切なものを 1 つ選べ。

(1) When Gulick said "It was a truly exciting moment when we first encountered the sediments from the impact itself and moreover when we realized we were seeing events in such detail," he mainly meant _____

   (a) studying rock rather than sediment is usually what geologists specialize in.

   (b) studying sediment and rock is not usually what geologists do.

   (c) the 130 meters of rock recorded events of the day the asteroid struck.

   (d) the 130 meters of rock was the record of a long period of time.

(2) Gulick and his team concluded that the asteroid must have vaporized all the sulfur that had previously existed inside the crater, because _____

   (a) much sulfur was found inside the crater, while rocks outside contained little sulfur.

   (b) no sulfur was found inside the crater, while rocks outside contained much sulfur.

   (c) rocks both inside and outside the crater contained little sulfur.

   (d) rocks both inside and outside the crater contained much sulfur.

EXERCISE 2 音声を聞き、下線部を補え。（2回録音されています。1回目はナチュラルスピード、2回目はスロースピードです。）

Natural
33

Slow
35

Global social distancing rules targeting coronavirus have pushed influenza infection rates to a record low, early figures show, signalling that the measures are (1) _____ other communicable diseases.

In China, where the earliest wide-scale lockdown measures began, new reports of diseases including mumps, measles and some sexually transmitted diseases, have declined significantly, though influenza cases (2) _____ . Infections reported monthly by the county's health ministry have dropped by over 90% since the beginning of the lockdown, from (3) _____ to 23,000.

Natural
34

Slow
36

Canada's flu surveillance system also reported "exceptionally low levels" of influenza in a recent report, (4) _____ weekly flu surveillance statistics including the UK and Australia. We've seen the lowest ever rates of other viral infection admissions for this time of year," said Ben Marais, an expert in infectious disease at the University of Sydney and clinician at the children's unit at Westmead Hospital. "We normally (5) _____ at this time of year, in winter…but this year the wards are essentially empty," he said.

The World Health Organisation (WHO) estimates there are some 3-5 million severe illnesses and up to 500,000 deaths annually linked to seasonal influenza globally. While experts say the drop in influenza infections has reduced the strain on healthcare systems and lowered the number of influenza fatalities, there's also concern that the unprecedented drop in cases could have a negative impact on immunity levels in following seasons.

— Based on a report on Reuters.com on July 31, 2020 —

〈ニュース解説〉 感染症の予防対策として social distancing（ソーシャル・ディスタンシング）が用いられたのは、世界各地で大流行したスペイン風邪（確定症例数5億人、死者数1700-5000万人）が大流行した1918年〜1921年に遡るといわれている。ただし、social distancing という表現が用いられたのは Merriam-Webster 辞典によると2003年とのこと。欧米など北半球の国々では秋から冬にかけてコロナ感染の第2波と共に、インフルエンザなどの季節性呼吸器ウイルス感染に襲われることが危惧されている。そうした中、本ニュースが伝える秋から冬の南半球における social distancing が他の感染症の抑制にも役立つとしたなら、朗報と言えよう。

(Notes)
rule 習慣、慣例 **communicable disease** 感染症、伝染病 **mumps** おたふく風邪 **measles** はしか **sexually transmitted disease** 性的感染症 **health ministry**（ここでは中華人民共和国）衛生部 **lockdown** 都市封鎖（lockdown は一つの建物などの「封鎖」の意味で用いられる場合もある）**flu surveillance system** インフルエンザ監視システム **admission** 入院 **Ben Marais** ベン・マレイス **University of Sydney** シドニー大学 **Westmead Hospital** ウェストミード病院 **World Health Organisation** 世界保健機関（本部：スイス・ジュネーブ）

■問A　空所 (a) ～ (f) にそれぞれ入るべき 1 語を下記の語群から選びその番号を記せ。

iPS（人工多能性幹）細胞	→	induced pluripotent (a) cell
タッチパネル	→	touch (b)
最先端の技術	→	(c)-of-the-art technology
高速増殖炉	→	fast breeder (d)
介護施設	→	nursing-(e) facility
生活習慣病	→	lifestyle-(f) disease

1. care	2. reactor	3. related
4. screen	5. state	6. stem

■問B　空所 (a) ～ (f) にそれぞれ入るべき 1 語を下記の語群から選びその番号を記せ。

遺伝子組み換え作物	→	genetically (a) crop
太陽光発電	→	(b) power generation
地上波デジタル放送	→	digital (c) broadcasting
医療過誤	→	medical (d)
平均寿命	→	average life (e)
介助犬	→	(f) dog

1. error	2. expectancy	3. modified
4. service	5. solar	6. terrestrial

■問C　(a) ～ (h) をそれぞれ和訳せよ。

(a) biodegradable plastic

(b) room-temperature superconductivity

(c) shape-memory garments

(d) capsule endoscope

(e) optical fiber

(f) heat stroke

(g) organ transplant

(h) brain death

Long, long, long wordy sentences — 長い、長い、長い冗漫な文体

小説や論説等でも長くて冗長な文章は敬遠される今日である。ましてや事件や出来事の報道を行うハード・ニュースの記事は正確で簡潔（precise and concise）が生命線。即時報道を目的としないフィーチャー・ニュース、即ち特集記事や読み物においてさえも、長くて取り留めのない文体はニュース記事では避けるべきである。一昔前までは英文で論理を展開する上では理想的な句や節と考えられていた表現方法、或いは過度な丁寧表現のように相手の立場に配慮した言い回しは、ストレートさが欠ける点で逆に文章内容をより複雑にして今日の読者に分かりにくくしている場合もある。ニュース英語のみならずビジネス英語でも同じような状況に遭遇するが、文章は説明口調ではなく簡潔さを保つことによってかえって伝える側の意図が迅速に且つ正確に読者に伝わることはしばしば指摘される。下の英文は、冗漫な文の典型例であるが、冗長な文体を避けるという本課の主旨からすると真逆の書き方でそのような文体を戒めているところが面白い。文章が lengthy 或いは wordy であるということは、退屈な（tedious）文章であることと表裏一体であることを忘れるべきではない。下の英文でも分かるように、文を長くするには様々な表現や方法があるが、文を短く正確に書くことは比較的難しい。

このトピックを英文で読んでみよう。

It should be pointed out that many writers, in order to make themselves sound much more profound and scholarly than perhaps they actually are, use flabby, inflated wording such as "it should be pointed out" and "in order to" and "perhaps"—which we just did ourselves, in fact, earlier in this sentence—in addition to piling up clauses (some using dashes such as those a few words back) or parentheses, such as those in the line above, not to mention semicolons, which often suggest that the writer wants to end the sentence but just cannot bring himself to actually type a period; nonetheless, today's busy readers are too impatient to tolerate the sort of 18th-century pomposity wherein writers, so in love with the sound of their own voices, just go on and on and on and on...

NEWS MEDIA IN THE WORLD

放送 Broadcasting (1)

✔ 20世紀初頭のラジオ、その後のテレビの発達を受け、放送ニュースは即時性と広域性を武器に成長。国際ニュース放送の老舗は英国 BBC（British Broadcasting Corporation）。世界中に広がる取材網を駆使、ラジオの World Service やテレビの BBC World で他をリードしてきた。米国 VOA（Voice of America）は米国国務省の対外宣伝部門として発足。冷戦時代には東側への西側意見の伝達役を担ったが、現在は、世界的なニュース専門機関の地位を確立している。

NEWS 14

What will Tokyo's postponed Olympics mean for Japanese politics?

Disk 2
37

"It is a problem that has happened every 40 years. It is the cursed Olympics," said Deputy Prime Minister Taro Aso in March, commenting on the then-imminent postponement of the 2020 Tokyo Summer Games. In 1940, Japan had planned to host the games, yet World War II forced Japan to cancel the Olympics, as was the case with the London games four years later. The Moscow Olympics 40 years later in 5 1980 saw the West boycott the competition due to the Soviet invasion of Afghanistan. Forty years later, in 2020, the Tokyo Olympics have been postponed to the summer of 2021 due to the COVID-19 pandemic.

The significance of the Olympic Games as an instrument for gaining prestige and a political and economic boost cannot be understated. The Berlin 1936, 10 Moscow 1980 and Los Angeles 1984 games were meant to serve as examples of each prevailing political system's superiority, while Athens 2004 and Rio 2016 were viewed as symbols of the host countries' rejuvenation. Likewise, the 2020 Tokyo Olympics are an attempt to cement Japan's status as a continuous economic powerhouse and a major actor on the international stage, but also to encapsulate the 15 legacy of Prime Minister Shinzo Abe and his Abenomics policies, implemented since 2012.

38

Upon returning to power eight years ago, Abe outlined an ambitious plan for Japan's future course after decades of stagnation, comprising the now-famous three arrows. In the realm of foreign policy, Japan was to pursue a global outlook, which to 20 date has best manifested itself in successful free trade policies. The largest bilateral trade pact ever between the EU and Japan was signed in 2018, and the year before, Abe rescued the Trans-Pacific Partnership, the viability of which had come under scrutiny after the United States' withdrawal.

However, it was not the first time that Japan's longest-serving prime minister 25 used his influence. He had played a personal role in pushing for Tokyo to be chosen to host the 2020 Olympics. It was Abe who intervened at the 2013 International Olympic Committee session to aid Tokyo's bid after concerns about safety had been raised due to the Fukushima nuclear disaster. The games would provide an ideal outlet to display to the global community Japan's resilience in the face of adversity, 30 while simultaneously boosting the nation's economic performance and achieving Abe's goal of preventing Japan from becoming a "tier two nation."

— Based on a report on Japantimes.com on May 8, 2020 —

〈ニュース解説〉 2020 年 3 月 25 日、新型コロナウィルス感染拡大が懸念される中、東京オリンピックの 2021 年夏への延期が決定された。自民党副総裁の「呪われたオリンピック 40 年周期」説も飛び出し、開催時期の延期は苦渋の選択であったが、裏返せばそれだけオリンピックの持つ政治的、経済的意味が大きいということで、日本の政治や経済にかなりの影響を及ぼすことが考えられる。

(Notes)

◆ (L. 1) **the cursed Olympics** 呪われたオリンピック（the Olympics は the Olympic Games とも呼ばれ、単数としても複数としても扱われる。複数の競技の集合体と考えるか、複数の競技が色々あると考えるかの違いである）

◆ (L. 2) **Deputy Prime Minister Taro Aso** 麻生太郎副総理（元首相で現財務大臣）

◆ (L. 6) **the Soviet invasion of Afghanistan** ソヴィエト連邦によるアフガニスタン侵攻（共産主義政党アフガニスタン人民民主党政権に対し、米国の援助を受けた武装勢力ムジャーヒディーンが蜂起。人民民主党政権の要請を受けたソヴィエト連邦が軍事介入。1989 年の撤退までに多数の死傷者を出した）

◆ (L. 10) **Berlin 1936** 1936 年のベルリン・オリンピック（「ヒトラーのオリンピック」とも言われるように、ナチスのプロパガンダに利用されたとの批判もある）

◆ (L. 10) **Moscow 1980** モスクワ・オリンピック（ソヴィエト連邦のアフガニスタン侵攻に抗議し、多くの国がボイコットした大会であった。政治とスポーツの関係が論じられた大会でもあった）

◆ (L. 11) **Los Angeles 1984** ロサンジェルス・オリンピック（放映権料やスポンサーからの高額の協賛金といった収入に加え、既存施設の使用等で支出を抑え、大きな黒字を産み出したこのオリンピックは、商業五輪の先駆けとも言われる）

◆ (L. 12) **Athens 2004** アテネ・オリンピック（アテネで五輪が開催されたのは、第 1 回大会に続いて 2 度目である）

◆ (L. 12) **Rio 2016** リオ・オリンピック（ブラジルのリオデジャネイロで開催。南アメリカ大陸で開催された最初のオリンピック）

◆ (L. 14) **economic powerhouse** 経済大国

◆ (L. 16) **Abenomics** アベノミクス（2012 年 12 月にスタートした第 2 次安倍内閣で掲げられた経済政策で、大胆な金融緩和、機動的な財政政策、民間投資を喚起する成長戦略のいわゆる 3 本の矢で、デフレ脱却を達成しようとした）

◆ (L. 18) **stagnation** 景気の停滞（いわゆる不況であるが、economic slump, recession, economic downturn 等と同義。the Depression は、1930 年代の世界的大不況である大恐慌を指すが、今回のコロナウィルス感染拡大による大不況は Corona Depression と称されることもある）

◆ (L. 20-21) **bilateral trade pact** 2 国間貿易協定（多国間は multilateral）

◆ (L. 22) **Trans-Pacific Partnership** 環太平洋経済連携協定（Trans-Pacific Partnership Agreement のことで、環太平洋パートナーシップ協定とも呼ばれる。環太平洋地域の国々の経済自由化を推進する目的で締結された経済連携協定。米国が当初の 12 締結国から離脱したため、11 か国で協定発効のため協議が行われ、米国抜きの体制で 2018 年に発効）

◆ (L. 26-27) **the 2013 International Olympic Committee session** 2013 年に開催された国際オリンピック委員会総会（アルゼンチンのブエノスアイレスで開催された第 125 回総会で、2020 年夏季オリンピックの開催地として東京が選ばれた）

◆ (L. 28) **Fukushima nuclear disaster** 福島原発事故

◆ (L. 31) **"tier two nation"** 2 等国（a nation of the second rank の意。Tier は段、列の意。tier one とか tier two はラグビーの世界でも使われる。ラグビーの統括団体であるワールドラグビーが発表する世界ランキングとは別に、ティアと呼ばれる階級が存在。Tier 1 は強豪国、Tier 2 は中堅国、Tier 3 は発展国であり、日本は 2019 年のラグビー・ワールドカップでの活躍もあり、Tier 1 に昇格した。本書 Chapter 15, News 15 参照）

1. 本文の内容と一致するものには T (True) を、一致しないものには F (False) を記せ。

(　　) (1) A comment made by Taro Aso was a major reason behind the decision to postpone the 2020 Tokyo Olympics.

(　　) (2) The 1944 London Olympic Games was cancelled due to World War II.

(　　) (3) All the supposedly cursed Olympics were cancelled because of the same type of disaster.

(　　) (4) The Olympic Games are often seen as a means of raising the prestige of a nation.

(　　) (5) The Olympic Games held in Berlin in 1936 were most likely politically motivated.

(　　) (6) The article seems to assume that Japan's status as an economic powerhouse is a thing of the past.

(　　) (7) The conclusion of the bilateral trade agreement between the EU and Japan became a harbinger of yet another trade treaty between Japan and the United States.

(　　) (8) The postponement of the 2020 Tokyo Olympics has a great deal to do with Washington's withdrawal from the TPP framework.

2. 次の英文を完成させるために、(a) 〜 (d) から最も適切なものを１つ選べ。

Prime Minister Shinzo Abe intervened during the 2013 International Olympic Committee session to support Tokyo's bid for the 2020 Summer Olympics because _____

(a) he wanted the world to know that his country had succeeded in restoring safety in Fukushima after the nuclear disaster.

(b) he thought the session was a good stage to promote his country to the status of a tier two nation.

(c) he wanted to show the world community how he himself managed to recover from hardship after the Fukushima nuclear disaster.

(d) he wanted to give a boost to Japan's economy which has been in a downturn trend since the introduction of Abenomics.

音声を聞き、下線部を補え。（２回録音されています。１回目はナチュラルスピード、２回目はスロースピードです。）

natural
39
Slow
41

The Nippon Professional Baseball season, which has been delayed by the coronavirus pandemic, will begin June 19, the league announced on Monday.

The 2020 campaign will (1)_____, though the league will continue to monitor the situation in hopes of allowing spectators into ballparks later in the summer. Opening day was originally scheduled for March 20 before being postponed because of the COVID-19 outbreak.

natural
40
Slow
42

While NPB teams normally (2)_____ _____, NPB Commissioner Atsushi Saito said clubs would be aiming to complete 120 during the shortened 2020 season. The commissioner said his office was "not too far away" from revealing the revised 2020 schedule. He hinted the schedule would be made in a way that (3)_____ _____ in regard to games, practices and travel.

It's also been speculated the NPB would (4)_____ or put a time limit on when a new inning could start, though Saito would only say the leagues "are discussing it." the NPB has already (5)_____ _____ as well as the annual All-Star Series.

— *Based on a report on Japantimes.com on May 25, 2020* —

5

10

15

〈ニュース解説〉　新型コロナウィルス感染拡大で開幕が延期になっていた日本プロ野球公式戦が無観客試合として6月19日にスタート。7月10日からは最大5千人を上限に観客を入れることが許可されるが、延長10回打ち切り制や1軍出場登録人数・ベンチ入り人数の増員等2020年特別ルールが制定される。コロナ禍の影響で、開幕後も例年とは違ったスケジュールや実施方法のシーズンとなった。

(Notes)
Nippon Professional Baseball season 日本野球機構公式戦（日本野球機構は NPB と略され、いわゆる日本プロ野球である）　**2020 campaign** 2020 年シーズン　**league** ここでは NPB のこと（league とは通常プロ野球の両リーグである Central League と Pacific League であるが、ここではサッカーの J リーグのように統括団体である日本野球機構を指す）　**commissioner** コミッショナー（プロスポーツの統括組織の最高責任者を指す。ここでは、日本野球機構の最高責任者）　**annual All-Star Series** 毎年恒例のオールスターゲーム

■問A 相撲で用いられる次の用語に対する英語表現を下記の語群から選びその番号を記せ。

(a) 寄り切り　　　(b) つり出し　　　(c) 上手投げ

(d) 下手投げ　　　(e) まげ　　　　　(f) 親方

(g) 押し出し　　　(h) 土俵入り　　　(i) 横綱

> 1. forcing out　　　2. grand champion　　3. lifting out
> 4. overarm throw　　5. pushing out　　　6. ring entering ceremony
> 7. stable master　　8. topknot　　　　　9. underarm throw

■問B (a)〜(g) の体操用語にそれぞれ対応する日本語表現を下記の語群から選びその番号を記せ。

(a) balance beam　　(b) floor exercise　　(c) flying rings　　(d) horse vault

(e) parallel bars　　(f) pommel horse　　(g) uneven bars

> 1. あん馬　　　2. 段違い平行棒　　3. 跳馬　　　4. つり輪
> 5. 平均台　　　6. 平行棒　　　　　7. ゆか

■問C 下記のそれぞれの語群の中から正しいものを選びその番号を記せ。

【サッカー用語】
　　　a. ロスタイム　　　→　1. injury time　　2. loss time
　　　b. シュート　　　　→　1. shoot　　　　　2. shot
　　　c. オウンゴール　　→　1. own goal　　　2. aun goal

【ゴルフ用語】
　　　d. ティーオフ　　　→　1. tea-off　　　　2. tee-off
　　　e. ボギー　　　　　→　1. bogey　　　　　2. bogy
　　　f. パー　　　　　　→　1. par　　　　　　2. per
　　　g. バーディー　　　→　1. bardie　　　　　2. birdie

【野球用語】
　　　h. コールドゲーム　→　1. called game　　2. cold game
　　　i. スクイズ　　　　→　1. squeeze bunt　　2. squiz bunt
　　　j. ライナー　　　　→　1. line drive　　　2. rhine drive
　　　k. ゴロ　　　　　　→　1. go-low　　　　　2. grounder
　　　l. フライ　　　　　→　1. fly　　　　　　　2. fry
　　　m. フォアボール　　→　1. base on balls　　2. four balls
　　　n. サウスポー　　　→　1. southpaw　　　　2. southpour
　　　o. ホームラン　　　→　1. homerun　　　　　2. home run

Jargon and journalese ― 専門用語とジャーナリズム調の文体

ニュースにとって最も重要なことは「分かりやすい」ことだ。誰もが忙しい現代、基本的に「読み捨て」される新聞記事は誰が読んでもきちんと内容が伝わること、いちいち読み返さなくても分かることが非常に重要だからである。英語の新聞の場合でも、難解な言葉や表現を避け、単語そのものもできるだけわかりやすい short words を用いる。例えば purchase → buy、attempt → try、anticipate → expect、utilize → use、request → ask、obtain → get などである。しかし、時に新聞記事は陳腐で大げさなジャーナリズム的表現に陥りがちであることも事実だ。

このトピックを英文で読んでみよう。

Bureaucrats love to use words like *utilize*, *finalize*, and *structured*. Cops like to say suspects are *apprehended* and *incarcerated*. And if you are a campus spokesman, why would you want to say "*the school can't afford to pay raises*" when you could say "*the salary scale revision will adversely affect the university's financial stability*"?

Good reporters relentlessly strive to filter out bloated, convoluted jargon and officialese. And those who do not should be *redirected*, *transitioned*, or *subject to personnel surplus reduction* (i.e., fired).

But reporters often lapse into "journalese" without realizing it. Journalese, as veteran editor Joe Grimm puts it, is the peculiar language that newspapers have evolved that reads like this:

Negotiators yesterday, in an eleventh-hour decision following marathon talks, hammered out an agreement on a key wage provision they earlier had rejected.

That's not as bad as bureaucratic gobbledygook. But it is still a problem, because it is still full of clichés.

NEWS MEDIA IN THE WORLD

放送 Broadcasting (2)

✔ 放送産業の故郷米国では、ラジオ放送についで、1940年代には商業テレビ放送が開始。CBS（Columbia Broadcasting System）、NBC（National Broadcasting Company）、ABC（American Broadcasting Company）の3大ネットワーク時代が続いたが、現在ではFOXを含め4大ネットワークと呼ばれることもある。さらに地上波放送に飽き足らない視聴者のニーズに応える形でケーブルテレビが急拡大。80年代にはCNN（Cable News Network）が衛星放送による世界初のニュース専門テレビ局として誕生。衛星放送が東側住民へ情報を提供し、冷戦終結に貢献したという評価もある。

NEWS 15

Disk 2

 Japan's national rugby team to be certified Tier 1

TOKYO—World Rugby, the sport's governing body, has decided to certify Japan as a Tier 1 country, making it the first Asian nation to ascend to the sport's top echelon. The decision comes days after Sir Bill Beaumont was reelected as World Rugby's chairman. Beaumont was in a tight race to keep his job against Agustin Pichot, and according to sources, he won Japan Rugby Football Union's backing with a promise 5 to promote the national team to Tier 1.

The chairman has also told the Japanese rugby union that a Lions Tour exhibition will be held in Japan, marking the first time for the team made up of the top players from the four UK states and Ireland to play in Japan. Tier 1 status will mean more games against other Tier 1 teams and more weight when rugby unions 10 vote on World Rugby matters. It could also lead to Japan receiving more World Rugby funds when budget money is distributed.

Tiers are a class system unique to rugby, with the top tier long consisting of 10 countries from Europe and the Southern Hemisphere. But the system is breaking down. Japan, for instance, has been in Tier 2 despite a combined record of 7-2 in the 15 last two Rugby World Cups. These results would put Japan in the middle of the Tier 1 pack. In addition, Japan was a top-eight finisher at the 2019 World Cup, which the country hosted to great acclaim.

The promotion to Tier 1 marks an important turning point in Japan's rugby history. It could give the sport a boost in Japan. While the game has a cult following 20 in the country, it had been losing its appeal for years before the 2019 World Cup. Tier 1 status could further rekindle interest in the game among young athletes and fans.

The Lions Tour exhibition is expected to be another boost. The tour is considered the sport's second biggest event, after the World Cup. It is held once every four years, with the games played somewhere in the Southern Hemisphere. Next year, the tour 25 will take place in South Africa. The exhibition against Japan's national team, which will precede the games in South Africa, is expected to attract a global audience.

— Based on a report on asia.nikkei.com on May 5, 2020 —

〈ニュース解説〉 日本で開催された 2019 年ラグビー・ワールドカップ（2019 Rugby World Cup）での日本代表の活躍もあり、日本はワールドラグビーのティア 1 国（Tier 1 country）に昇格することになった。日本は 11 番目のティア 1 国になり、強豪国との試合設定や、分配金の受け取り等で有利な立場を維持できることとなった。これまでティア 1 国は、ラグビー・チャンピオンシップに参戦する南半球 4 か国（ニュージーランド、オーストラリア、南アフリカ、アルゼンチン）とシックス・ネイションズ・チャンピオンシップを戦う欧州 6 か国（イングランド、フランス、アイルランド、スコットランド、ウェールズ、イタリア）の合計 10 か国から構成されるラグビー強豪国を指した。

(Notes)

◆ (L. 1) **World Rugby**　ワールドラグビー（ラグビーの国際統括団体）

◆ (L. 2) **echelon**　階層、階級、レベル

◆ (L. 3) **Sir Bill Beaumont**　サー・ビル・ボーモント［元イングランド代表主将で現ワールドラグビー会長。サーは英国の叙勲制度の称号の 1 つで、ナイト爵（knight、騎士爵）の意。敬称として用いられる］

◆ (L. 4) **Agustin Pichot**　アグスティン・ピチョット（元アルゼンチン代表。ワールドラグビー副会長。2007 年ワールドカップではアルゼンチン代表主将として第 3 位獲得に貢献した）

◆ (L. 5) **Japan Rugby Football Union**　日本ラグビーフットボール協会

◆ (L. 7) **Lions Tour**　ライオンズ・ツアー（ブリティッシュ＆アイリッシュ・ライオンズ・ツアーのことで、英国とアイルランドのラグビー 4 協会であるイングランド、スコットランド、ウェールズ、アイルランドの代表選手から 4 年に 1 度選手が選抜され編成されるチーム。南半球の強豪国との試合が行われる。アイルランド・ラグビー協会は、アイルランドが南北に分かれる前からの協会であったため、アイルランド共和国と英国の北アイルランドの両方から選手が選抜される。2021 年夏は 2019 年ラグビー・ワールドカップ優勝国南アフリカ共和国への遠征が予定されている。Exhibition はツアー前に行われるとされるライオンズと日本代表との公開試合である）

◆ (L. 10) **rugby unions**　ラグビー協会（ここでは各国のラグビー協会を指す。本来ラグビーユニオンとは、一般にラグビーと呼ばれる 15 人制のラグビーユニオンのことである。1895 年にラグビーは、このラグビーユニオンとそこから離脱したラグビーリーグに分かれた。後者は 1 チーム 13 人でプレーし、ルールも前者とはかなり違う）

◆ (L. 13) **class system**　階級制度

◆ (L. 16) **last two Rugby World Cups**　直近 2 回のラグビー・ワールドカップ（具体的には 2019 年の日本大会、2015 年のイングランド大会）

　ニュースを読んで、下記の設問に答えよ。

1. 本文の内容と一致するものには T (True) を、一致しないものには F (False) を記せ。

(　　　) (1) The decision to promote Japan to a Tier 1 country was the result of the Japanese government's ceaseless campaign.

(　　　) (2) The article suggests that the promotion of Japan to the Tier 1 status has had a great deal to do with Japan's support for Bill Beaumont during the election for World Rugby chairman.

(　　　) (3) The Japanese Rugby Union was happy to hear the news of Japan's promotion to Tier 1, but their joy was smothered almost immediately after hearing the news of an exhibition match against the Lions.

(　　　) (4) The Lions is made up of the top players from England and Scotland.

(　　　) (5) The countries belonging to Tier 1 have obvious advantages over those in the lower tiers.

(　　　) (6) Japan's record in the last two World Cups had some bearing on the country's advancement to the Tier 1.

(　　　) (7) In the Northern Hemisphere, Japan is the only powerhouse in the world of rugby.

(　　　) (8) One of the problems facing Japanese rugby had been the lack of dedicated fans for a long time.

(　　　) (9) Among the countries in the Southern Hemisphere, the Lions Tour seems to have more esteem and prestige than the Rugby World Cup.

(　　　) (10) The Lions Tour is a tour conducted by the winner of the last World Cup and played against the World Selection team.

2. 次の説明に相当するラグビー用語を下記の語群から選び、その語を空所に入れよ。

(a) The eight forwards from each team binding together and pushing against each other (　　　)

(b) The area where a player must remain for a minimum of 10 minutes after being shown a yellow card (　　　)

(c) An offence whereby a player deliberately impedes an opponent who does not have the ball (　　　)

(d) A charge executed on a player who has already passed or kicked away the ball (　　　)

(e) A contest to gain control over the ball, usually following a tackle, when the ball is on the ground and players from two opposing teams meet over the ball (　　　)

(f) The player who usually wears jersey number 15 and acts as the last line of defence (　　　)

1. fullback　2. late tackle　3. obstruction　4. ruck　5. scrum　6. sin bin

音声を聞き、下線部を補え。（２回録音されています。１回目はナチュラルスピード、２回目はスロースピードです。）

Natural
45
Slow
47

Tennis star Roger Federer is (1)
_____, according to Forbes. The 38-year-old earned a total of $106.3 million over the past 12 months, making him the first tennis player to top Forbes' world's 100 highest-paid athletes list. Athletes from 10 sports and 21 different countries made the list this year, but only two women made the cut— (2) 5
_____ since 2016.

Federer leapfrogs football stars Cristiano Ronaldo and Lionel Messi to secure top spot. The coronavirus pandemic triggered salary cuts for soccer stars Messi and Ronaldo, (3) _____ to rank as the world's highest-paid athlete for the first time. 10

Natural
46
Slow
48

Rising tennis star Naomi Osaka placed 29th, whilst her rival Serena Williams was 33rd. However, Osaka becomes the highest-paid female athlete in history after earning $37.4 million over the last year. (4) _____ through a combination of prize money and endorsements.

Forbes' list takes into consideration factors such as prize money, salaries and endorsements from June 1, 2019. Salaries and endorsement income have skyrocketed in the past decade, but both are headed for precipitous falls, as (5) _____ and companies tighten their marketing budgets. 15

— *Based on a report on CNN.com on May 30, 2020* —

〈ニュース解説〉 米国経済誌『フォーブス』の2020年スポーツ選手長者番付によると、テニスプレーヤーのロジャー・フェデラーが、テニスプレーヤーとしては初めてのトップの座を占めた。サッカーのスーパースターであるクリスティアーノ・ロナウドやリオネル・メッシを抑えてのトップであり、ここにも新型コロナウィルス感染拡大の影響が出ている。日本からは大坂なおみが女子アスリートのトップを獲得したが、女子アスリートでトップ100に入ったのは、大坂とセリーナ・ウィリアムズのわずか2名であった。

(Notes)

Roger Federer ロジャー・フェデラー［スイスのプロテニス選手。サーブ、ボレー、ストロークとすべてに優れたオールラウンダー。4大大会（グランドスラム）最多優勝回数等多くの記録を持つ］ **Forbes** フォーブス誌（米国の経済誌。世界長者番付で知られ、本記事は同誌掲載のスポーツ選手の長者番付の結果に基づく） **make the cut** 枠に入る（ここではスポーツ選手長者番付100人に入ること。野球では登録選手枠に入ること、ゴルフでは予選を通過して決勝ラウンドに進むことを指す） **leapfrog** 飛び越す **Cristiano Ronaldo** クリスティアーノ・ロナウド（ポルトガル代表のサッカー選手。長くスペインのレアルマドリードでプレーしたが、現在はイタリア・セリエAのユベントスFC所属） **Lionel Messi** リオネル・メッシ（アルゼンチン代表のサッカー選手。2020年9月現在スペインリーグのFCバルセロナでプレーする。2019年のスポーツ選手長者番付ではトップであった） **Naomi Osaka** 大坂なおみ（大阪市出身で、アジア初のWTA世界ランキング1位を獲得したプロテニス選手。2018年の全米、2019年の全豪で優勝） **Serena Williams** セリーナ・ウィリアムズ（女子テニス界にパワーテニスを持ち込んだ米国のプロテニス選手。グランドスラム優勝回数多数） **endorsement** （テレビ等での商品の）宣伝、コマーシャル

■問A (a)～(i) にそれぞれ対応する英語表現を下記の語群から選びその番号を記せ。

(a) 円盤投げ   (b) 砲丸投げ   (c) やり投げ

(d) ハンマー投げ   (e) 走高跳び   (f) 走幅跳び

(g) 三段跳び   (h) 棒高跳び   (i) 十種競技

1. decathlon	2. discus throw	3. hammer throw
4. high jump	5. javelin throw	6. long jump
7. pole vault	8. shot put	9. triple jump

■問B (a)～(h) の野球用語の説明に対応する英語を下記の語群から選びその番号を記せ。

(a) The extension of a baseball game until one team is ahead of the other at the end of an inning

(b) An out resulting from a batter getting three strikes during a time at bat

(c) Getting two players out on one play

(d) An act of deliberately hitting a baseball gently without swinging the bat so that it does not roll far into the infield

(e) A pitch that the catcher should have caught but missed, allowing runners to advance to the next base

(f) A relief pitcher who specializes in protecting a lead by getting the final outs in a close game

(g) A way of measuring a pitcher's effectiveness

(h) A pitch of a baseball that does not travel straight, as it is thrown with spin so that its path curves as it approaches the batter

1. breaking ball	2. bunt	3. closer	4. double play
5. earned run average	6. extra innings	7. passed ball	8. strikeout

Clichés（クリシェ）— 使い古された常套句

クリシェ（cliché）はフランス語語源で、「使い古され手垢がついてしまった陳腐な常套句」を意味する。元々は目新しくインパクトのある表現だったが、あまりにも使われすぎたため陳腐化してしまった比喩、イディオム、キャッチフレーズ、（聖書、文学作品、映画のセリフ等からの）引用、ことわざ、外来語、流行語などが含まれる。ライターの頭の中にはクリシェが定着してしまっているので、ニュースを書く際にも安易に、あるいは、無意識にクリシェを使ってしまいがちである。しかし、クリシェの使用は文を空疎で魅力のないものにしてしまう危険性があるので、できるだけ回避するのが望ましいとされている。*The New York Times Manual of Style and Usage* でも、「クリシェを用いる場合にはそれらを用いることに妥当性があるか否か（whether their use can be justified）を慎重に検討すべきだが、大抵の場合、その使用に妥当性はない」としている。クリシェと思われる表現をニュースの中で使おうとする場合には、その適切性・新鮮味をきちんと吟味することが必須である。*News Reporting and Writing*（Menche, 1987）によると、英国の作家でジャーナリストでもある George Orwell（ジョージ・オウェル）も、「印刷物で見慣れた表現を使用する時には常に慎重に」とライターに警告している。

このトピックを英文で読んでみよう。

Beyond the shadow of a doubt, you should work 24/7 to avoid clichés like the plague. Hel-*lo*? It's a no-brainer. Go ahead—make my day.

Tired, worn-out clichés instantly lower the IQ of your writing. So do corny newswriting clichés (a form of journalese) like these:

> The *close-knit community* was *shaken by the tragedy*.
>
> *Tempers flared over a laundry list of complaints*.
>
> The *embattled mayor* is *cautiously optimistic*, but *troubled youths* face an *uncertain future* sparked by *massive blasts* in *bullet-riddled, shark-infested waters*.
>
> So *now begins the heartbreaking task of cleaning up*.

Yes, clichés *can* come in handy. And yes, a skilled writer can use them in clever ways. Once in a blue moon.

NEWS MEDIA IN THE WORLD

放送 Broadcasting (3)

✓　CNN の成功を受け、90 年代以降ニュース専門チャンネルが続々登場。米国では、映像産業から派生した米国 FOX ニュースが参入。中東カタールにはアル・ジャジーラ（Al Jazeera）が誕生。インターネットとの融合による映像情報サービスの拡大を背景に、既存ニュース・メディアも含めた世界大のメディアミックス競争が進行中だ。

参考文献

R.E. Garst & T.M. Bernstein, *Headlines and Deadlines*, Columbia University Press (1963)

L.A. Campbell & R.E. Wolseley, *How to Report and Write the News*, Prentice-Hall (1961)

Tim Harrower, *Inside Reporting*, McGraw-Hill (2009)

The Missouri Group, *News Reporting and Writing*, Bedford / St Martins (2010)

William E. Blundell, *The Art and Craft of Feature Writing based on The Wall Street Journal Guide*, Plume (1988)

Darrell Christian, *The Associated Press Stylebook 2010 and Briefing on Media Law*, Associated Press (2010)

Rene J. Cappon, *The Associated Press Guide to News Writing*, 3rd ed., ARCO (2005),

Bill Kovach & Tom Rosenstiel, *The Elements of Journalism*, Three Rivers Press (2007)

Allan M. Siegal and William G. Connolly, *The New York Times Manual of Style and Usage*, Three Rivers Press (1999)

Paul R. Martin, (2002), *The Wall Street Journal Essential Guide to Business Style and Usage*, Free Press (2002)

Thomas W. Lippman, *The Washington Post Desk-Book on Style*, 2nd ed., McGraw-Hill (1989)

Brian S. Brooks & James L. Pinson, *Working with Words*, 2nd ed., St. Martin,s Press (1993)

Carole Rich, *Writing and Reporting News*, 5th ed., Thomson Wadsworth (2002)

藤井章雄，『放送ニュース英語　音を読む』，朝日出版社（1983）

藤井章雄，『ニュース英語がわかる本』，PHP 研究所（1992）

藤井章雄，『ニュース英語の翻訳プロセス』，早稲田大学出版部（1996）

藤井章雄，『放送ニュース英語の体系』，早稲田大学出版部（2004）

日本英語コミュニケーション学会紀要　第 7 巻（1998），8 巻（1999），11 巻（2002），12 巻（2003），13 巻（2004），15 巻（2006），17 巻（2008），18 巻（2009），19 巻（2010），20 巻（2011），21 巻（2012），22 巻（2013）

時事英語の総合演習
─ 2021 年度版 ─

検印
省略

© 2021年1月31日　第1版発行

編著者　　　堀江　洋文
　　　　　　加藤　香織
　　　　　　小西　和久
　　　　　　宮崎　修二
　　　　　　内野　泰子

発行者　　　原　　雅久

発行所　　　株式会社　朝日出版社
　　　101-0065　東京都千代田区西神田 3-3-5
　　　　　　電話　東京 (03)3239-0271
　　　　　　FAX　東京 (03)3239-0479
　　　e-mail　text-e@asahipress.com
　　　　　　振替口座　00140-2-46008
　　　組版／製版・信毎書籍印刷株式会社

ISBN 978-4-255-15665-1　C 1082